DAVID FORRESTER

CW01523853

WILSON'S HANDBOOK TO MORPETH

AND NEIGHBOURHOOD ILLUSTRATED

WITH WOODCUTS

NEWGATE PRESS, MORPETH
ISBN 0 9528793 0 1

First published in 1966 by David Forrester
Wilson . 8 Newgate Street Morpeth.
This enlarged facsimile edition published in 1996 by
Newgate Press, Morpeth,
60, Newgate Street Morpeth,
Northumberland.

PREFACE TO THE SECOND EDITION.

THE first edition of the HANDBOOK TO MORPETH having met with success, the Publisher has been induced to issue a second one, which has been considerably augmented, and the events brought down to the present time.

In order that this small work should have a large circulation, he has made a reduction in the price thereof, so as to bring it within the reach of any one wishing to gain some information regarding the Ancient Borough of Morpeth.

June, 1884.

INTRODUCTION.

IT will be acknowledged by every candid and impartial observer of social and commercial progress, that the ancient town of Morpeth has considerably increased in importance during the past 20 or 30 years. The railways, the telegraphs, and the press have all tended to develop the resources and the capabilities of the adjoining district, with its great mineral wealth, and Morpeth has experienced a share of the results of the mighty changes which have been wrought in the country by the introduction of the railway system. It is an important centre of connection by rail, forming the first town of note north of Newcastle, on the main line of the North-Eastern Railway, which passes by Morpeth to the North. On the east is the coast line of the Blyth and Tyne section of the North-Eastern Railway, and on the west is the Wansbeck Valley branch, which joins the main line at Morpeth, and its other terminus is at Reedsmouth, where it forms a junction with the Waverley route of the North British Railway Company. The line also communicates by a branch with Rothbury, which is visited by large numbers of excursionists as well as Morpeth.

The town and trade of Morpeth has thus greatly improved within the last 30 years. A few of the most ancient buildings and places of business still remain conspicuous in the front streets, but the greater portion have been altered and improved to the more business-like appearance of the present time. Still, here and there may be seen the old-fashioned house, with its overhanging upper storeys, or quaintly-shaped roof.

The borough of Morpeth, however, stands among the foremost towns of the county for its charming scenery, and it has long been one of the choice resorts of excursionists at holiday times, and a large number of visitors frequent the town during the summer season. In the absence of a Guide to the district, it is probable that a number of the shady woods and the extent of the pleasant footpaths and walks which branch off on all sides are unknown to the majority of the casual visitors to the ancient borough; and with a view to assist those who desire to enjoy the beautiful scenery of the locality, and possess a little knowledge of the chief objects of interest in the neighbourhood, the following notes are tendered.

MORPETH.

THE ancient Borough of Morpeth is pleasantly situated
in the vale of the Wansbeck, and is 17 miles north
of Newcastle by rail, and 14 miles by road. It is surrounded by grassy slopes crowned by fine stretches of
picturesque copse and woodland. The Wansbeck flows
past the town on the west, south, and east sides, and adds
greatly to the beauty of the scenery of the district. It is
said to have its rise in a bog between Airdlaw and the Great
and Little Waneyhouse Crags; runs in pools down Russell
Dene, and thence through Sweethope Lough, taking in the
Rayburn at Whelpington, the Hart at Hartburn, and the
Font at Mitford, From the mill weir on the Mitford Road
it runs by the steep heights which rise almost perpendi-
cularly on the north side, and which are studded with tall
and majestic trees. It then pursues its lively career by the
gardens, the High Stanners—skirts the Castle Wood and
the banks of the south side, thence by the town and the
Low Stanners, through the lovely Bothal Wood, thence by
Bothal, Sheepwash, Stakeford and North Seaton, and enters
the German Ocean at the north side of Cambois.

The following brief sketch of the town and the walks
in its vicinity, was communicated to the *Newcastle Weekly
Chronicle* by the compiler, and will convey an idea of the
direction of the various paths in the neighbourhood, from

the Castle Hills, a delightfully situated stretch of land on the south side of the river Wansbeck, access to which is gained by Hillgate, a narrow street to the left of the entrance to Morpeth, before crossing the bridge to the town : and access is also gained to the hills from the high end of Bridge Street, by Oldgate, over the foot bridge, and through the Castle Wood.

"THE ENTRANCE TO THE TOWN

is strikingly beautiful, and the objects brought before the eye in the descent from the railway station are really fascinating. Apart from the magnificent beech, ash, and fir trees which overhang the roadway facing the visitor, and which constitutes a delightful avenue on each side of the road leading to the town, there is, opposite the descent from the Station, at a high elevation, the ruins of the Castle of Morpeth. The gateway (now restored and inhabited by the local agent of the Earl of Carlisle) of the old castle, supposed to have been built in the reign of William the Conqueror by William de Merlay, may be observed through the trees, and a portion of the walls, erected in the eleventh or twelfth century, is all that remains of the castle. Near the town, is the noble building with its castellated towers, the County Prison, better known to almost every person in this part of the county as Morpeth Gaol, but which is now empty in consequence of the prisoners having been removed to Newcastle.

"Morpeth is blessed, or rather favoured, with county institutions. About a mile or so, as the crow flies, from the elevation of the Railway Station to the elevation opposite, in a north-easterly direction, is a a handsome building —the County Lunatic Asylum—which is easily discernible by the bright red colour of the bricks with which it is built,

and its commanding position, on the brow of the hill, at
Cottingwood. It is beautifully surrounded on three sides
with woods. Before crossing. either of the bridges which
admit the visitor to the chief business part of the borough,
on the left is a narrow street, which leads in a westerly
direction to the Castle Hills. Up Hillgate, on the south
side of the river, or the side of the river on which the
Castle and Gaol are situated, a hundred yards' walk intro-
duces the visitor to the beautiful slopes which overlook the
town, and the vale of the Wansbeck, an excellent view of
which has been published by Mr. Wilson, of Morpeth, in
tinted lithography, from a drawing by an eminent London
artist.

CHIEF BUILDINGS.

" From the Castle Hills can be easily observed the chief
buildings of the town. The Morpeth Free Grammar School
(a charity of King Edward the Sixth, granted by charter
dated 1552) is a comparatively recent erection, beyond the
central part of the town, in the fields to the left below the
Asylum. The Roman Catholic Church of St. Robert is in
Oldgate Street, to the west of the old Clock Tower, and at
the latter, even now,
          ' The curfew tolls the knell of parting day.'
The Established Church of St. James is in the back part of
the town, and is approached from Newgate Street by a
splendid avenue of trees, a little below Copper Chare. At
the bridge end, on the right, a most prominent feature is the
steeple of the late Dr. Anderson's Church, as it is generally
called, or more properly, perhaps, St. George's English
Presbyterian Church, which was erected on the site of
what was known as the old Town's Mill, about twenty-
four years since. On the other side of the Bridge are the

remains of the Morpeth Chapel of All Saints and a Chantry, built prior to 1300, now occupied by Mr. Young as an Erated Water Manufactory. To the left of the visitor seated on the hills and looking towards the town, and opposite the High Stanners, is situated the Union Workhouse, conspicuous by the red bricks with which it is built. The Town Hall, as it is termed, is in the centre of the town, at the junction of the two main thoroughfares— Bridge Street and Newgate Street—which comprise the entrances to the town from the south and north turnpikes respectively.

BEAUTIFUL WOODS AND WALKS.

" The Castle Hills, as before stated, are pleasantly situated, and to the right, or behind the entrance below the Castle is the ' Ha Hill,' or High Hill, a very high circular mound, with a flat top, supposed to have been erected artificially for protection in times of war. The wood behind the hawthorn-covered hedges at the summit of the hills, is known as the Postern, from which is a fine green slope to a deep valley below, through which in olden times ran the water of the Castle moat. The beautiful footpaths along each side of the valley are public, and the people are at liberty to pass along and over the nicely-laid out gravel roads through the gates and wicket past the Castle gateway, and on to the old castle road which takes down to the stairs which are seen on the turnpike a little above the Gaol on going from the Station. The wicket and gates at the Castle footpaths will be found open, and the visitor will meet with no barrier or notice of prosecution for trespass in passing through and along the gravel carriage roads, which take to the right and left. On the Castle banks, some of the finest little open woods in the country are to be seen on every side. At the high end of the hills is the Castle Wood, and further on, upon a level above the wood-and-iron Bridge, is the High Stanners, on which cricketers play nightly during the season.

" On the north side of the River to the east, on the turnpike leading in the direction of Pegswood and Longhirst, are the banks near the Asylum, known as the 'Mount Hags,' above which, approached by a footpath from the turnpike, is a small forest known as the Blue Bell Wood, through which a beautiful path leads to a second wood familiarly termed ' Willie Booman's Wood.'

" Below the Gaol is a narrow lane, called the Goose Hill, which conducts to a delightful walk close by the river side, known as ' Bennett's Walk.' This leads to the Bore Hole Lane. The Bore Hole, which adjoins a cottage surrounded by pretty little garden plots, is where a party were boring for coal, when the water burst out in such a volume that the sinkers had to desist. The water is economised in a large, square bath, built of stone, some four or five yards in diameter, and is enclosed and used for bathing at the charge of a penny. Thence this footpath passes on to the quarry drift, and another path leads onward and up the bank, revealing a grand view of the town and the Wansbeck Valley, and the path takes to the Park House, on the Station road, or Coopie's Lane. The Local Board of Health has put up several substantial stiles on these paths, and the visitor can pass on for some distance as he chooses.

" At the Quarry Drift, however, the visitor can turn to the left. Crossing the wood bridge, and pursuing the turnpike for the matter of a couple of hundred yards up the bank, he will reach a gate, which is the entrance to the famous Lady's Chapel Wood, through which a fine picturesque path by the river side leads almost to Bothal. About a mile and a half down the wood, a few stones to the left of the path are nearly all that remain of what was once the Lady's Chapel. Close by was the well, it is said, from whence was procured the holy water for the font. One Rector of Bothal, of a benevolent turn, is said to have had a splendid collection of flowers planted and cultivated near the chapel ruins, and a rustic seat was cut out with a ledge overhanging it, as a protection from the oppressive rays of the sun, or a shelter from the passing shower, and overhead, upon or beside the ledge, was put up the following, or a rhyme to similar effect :—

> ' Rest, weary pilgrim, at the well,
> But do not pluck the flowers ;
> They do not grow for you alone
> Amongst these pretty bowers.'

" There are numerous other paths—by the Allery Banks, over the high wood foot-bridge erected accross the railway, is a path leading to Choppington ; and another proceeds by the Terrace behind the church at the Bridge end past the Low Stanners (which are to be improved and planted with trees), by the Waulk Mill Field, and thus to the Asylum road, &c. But let us briefly allude to the attractions in the direction of Mitford.

" The visitor may turn his steps through the Castle Wood at the west end of the Castle Banks, and proceed past the High Stanners, to a lovely footpath which leads by the border wall of the river to Mitford Bridge. To the left of the turnpike road, or farm road, which skirts the ruins of Newminster Abbey, will be observed the only part remaining of the abbey, which is the porch, enclosed by a paling. The narrow road-way leads to the Kennels through fields past the Abbey Mills, and a path also takes through the Borough Wood to the ruins of Old Mitford Castle, and to Mitford Church, which has been rebuilt. A footpath entering by the lane below the Mitford Bridge, leads up the bank and by the fields to Spital Hill and Peacock Gap, on the north turnpike.

"There are two pleasant paths running through the Castle Wood—the one leading from the top of the wood to the Cemetery, and the old parish church of Morpeth, St. Mary's, opposite which is the vicarage and residence of the rector, the Hon. and Rev. F. R. Grey. This is a delightful walk, and a favourite with many of the visitors and residents. The other path at the far end of the wood, called the 'Curlykews,' leads by the fields to Morpeth Common, or, instead of turning to the left to the Common, the path may be followed to the right, across a plank over a narrow ravine, and thence along the top of the meadows sloping down to the Kennels and Abbey at the Mitford road.

"The main Bridge at the entrance of the town was built in 1831, and has greatly added to the beauty and advantage of the borough. The iron and wood Foot Bridge, approached by the narrow street to the left—Wansbeck Street—was built in 1869, on the site and pillars of the ancient bridge, over which the mail coaches between London and Edinburgh ran. The old bridge was blown up some years ago. At the High Stanners is another iron and wood Foot Bridge, built on the site of the suspension bridge which broke down and injured several persons on the band festival day only a few years back. A little higher up is a Wood Bridge leading over the river, to the north side, but before reaching the village of Mitford, the Wansbeck has to be crossed by 3 more bridges, or in all 6 within a distance of two miles."

————o————

To the above may be added the following general remarks respecting the town :—The chief thoroughfares are named Bridge Street and Newgate Street, at the junction of which is the Market Place, and from which branches off towards the river, by the Clock Tower, the street called Oldgate. Some distance up Newgate Street, is a street of fair proportions, which takes off to the right, called Manchester Street, in which is the Wesleyan Chapel, and at its extremity is the neat little chapel used by the Primitive Methodist body as their place of worship. Further up Newgate Street, is Copper Chare, which shows a marked improvement in the character of its buildings contrasted with those of which it was formerly the site. Several new houses have been erected, and in the centre of the chare is the new Masonic Hall, which will be noticed more particularly hereafter. One then passes on through the main street to the "top of the town," or to the township of Bullersgreen, to the left of which is the Dogger Bank, leading to Mitford, and on the right is the turnpike road to the North. At the entrance to the town, to the right of the bridge, by the Church of St. George, is the road directing to Bothal, Pegswood, and Longhirst. It is only, however, from the elevated heights of the Castle Hills or the summit of the slopes which shelter the town on every side, that the narrow streets and lanes, with their old brick houses and tiled roofs, can be seen diverging from the main streets by entrances which would otherwise be unnoticed by the stranger to the town. A number of yards and lanes enter from the main streets, and are densely populated. In a sanitary point of view, however, the yards and lanes are kept in a very cleanly and healthy state by the residents. A narrow lane, known as the "Back Way," will be seen threading its way through behind the front streets, and by the top of the lanes, to the road passing the foot of the town near the Dam Side. The large ironworks of Messrs. Swinney Brothers, the extensive brewery buildings of Mr. Loades, and the new brewery of Messrs. Hopper and Anderson, are to be seen at the various points in the neighbourhood of the Back Way. A fine row of buildings at the back of the ancient borough, facing the fields sloping from Cottingwood, is termed Howard Terrace; between the town and this terrace is Dacre Street, in which several dwellings of a superior character are erected.

THE NAME OF MORPETH.

Many years ago Morpeth was universally spelt Morepath, and Hodgson gives it as his opinion that this name became attached to the town in consequence of its being situated on the path across the moor. This seems the most sensible derivation of the name that could be found, and it is infinitely more feasible than the speculation of Camden, who fancies that Morpeth was originally the famous Roman station of Corstopitum. He argues that the name Corstopitum might have been substituted by Morstipitum, and this name having by frequent repetition become affixed to the town, would by degrees become abbreviated and transformed into Morpit or Morpeth. Horsley, however, in his "Britannia Romana," plainly shows Corbridge to be the seat of the ancient Corstopitum, and he makes no mention of any evidence of the Romans having inhabited Morpeth, and in the absence of any such evidence, and with a name of pure Saxon origin, it is much safer to assume that Morpeth, at the time of the Romans, was covered with wood or moorland.

THE POPULATION OF MORPETH.

The population of the municipal borough, in 1871, was 4,590, and in 1881, 5,068, showing an increase of nearly 500. The parliamentary borough was extended considerably between the periods named—hence, in 1871, the population of the Parliamentary district was 30,189, and in 1881, 33,402.

THE CORPORATION OF MORPETH.

Morpeth is a corporate borough, and is governed by a Council numbering 12 members, and 4 aldermen who are chosen by the former. Four councillors are elected annually, and sit for the period of three years. The Mayor for the time being presides over the Borough Petty Sessions Court and is generally assisted by the ex-mayor or by a county magistrate, according to circumstances. Two aldermen are chosen by the Council every three years, and hold office for six years. The mayor is chosen annually by the Council from their number.

As is gathered from several ancient documents in possession of the corporation, Morpeth is a borough by prescription, which is an evidence of its antiquity. Morpeth, however, has a charter granted to it by Charles II., but the town had been incorporated for centuries prior to 1662, and possesses charters of very ancient date. The earliest dated deeds in the Hutch of the corporation are said to be of the time of Edward I., whose reign commenced in 1272, and it is thought that other deeds, undated, but having the seal of the town attached, are those of a still more ancient period. There was also a charter granted by Roger de Merlay the

3rd, who was baron of Morpeth from 1239 to 1266, by which he granted lands and tenements in Morpeth to his free burgesses of Morpeth, and Hodgson refers to a charter granted to the burgesses by Roger de Merlay the 2nd, who succeeded his father in 1188, between this date and 1239, by which he gave to his free burgesses all the liberties and free customs, as he himself enjoyed in the barony, as granted by the Crown. So much having been said on the matter of the establishment of the corporation, there is nothing to the contrary to show that it has not existed ever since without intermission. A number of deeds testify its existence from that distant period until now, when the municipal authority is in a most vigorous and thriving condition.

THE POLITICAL HISTORY OF MORPETH.

The political history of Morpeth dates as far back as 1352, when a writ was issued by Edward III. summoning Lord Greystock to attend him in Parliament at Westminster. The first election of members for Morpeth was in the year 1553, when two elections took place, one in the spring before Edward VI. died, and the other in the autumn after the commencement of Mary's reign. From this time to 1832, when the Reform Bill passed, the borough had been represented by two members, but, with its now enlarged boundaries, it had but one member, in the person of Captain F. G. Howard. On the death of this gentleman in 1833, the seat was represented by the Hon. E. G. G. Howard, who retired in 1837, when Lord Levison, now Earl Granville, Secretary for Foreign Affairs, was returned for the seat. The latter retired in 1840, when the former member, the Hon. E. G. G. Howard, resumed the representation of the Borough. In 1852, Sir George Grey, being defeated in

North Northumberland, the retirement of Mr. Howard gave
him the vacancy at Morpeth. Sir George Grey, having
been appointed Secretary of State for the Colonies, was
re-elected in 1854, and was also re-elected as Chancellor of
the Duchy of Lancaster in 1859, and as Home Secretary in
1861. The Reform Act of 1867 still further enlarged the
limits of the borough of Morpeth, and Sir George Grey
continued to represent it until the dissolution in 1874, a
period of 22 years. In 1872 a movement was begun with
a view of obtaining the franchise for the miners. Their
object was to secure the return of Mr. Thomas Burt to
Parliament as the working man's representative. After
several struggles and determined efforts to have their rights
recognised, at the Revision Court held at Morpeth on the
27th of September, 1873, the lists prepared by the over-
seers were passed by the Revising Barrister, and the miners
reaped the reward of their perseverance, and became a
power in the State. At the first registration of the extended
borough the total number of electors was 1,698. Of this
number, Blyth and Newsham sent 166, and Cowpen 373,
the remaining 1,159 being furnished by Bedlington and
Morpeth in about equal proportions. In 1872 the number
on the list had increased to 2,661, of which number Morpeth
and its dependent villages contributed 780, Bedlington
1,207, Cowpen 361, and Newsham and Blyth 306. The
number of voters in the borough in September, 1873, was
4,916, being an increase of 2,255, as compared with the
previous year. Morpeth had increased its proportions by
only 24, standing now at 804; Bedlington has nearly doubled
its constituency, its figures being 2,244, while Cowpen, with
1,377, has almost quadrupled the number of its electors,
and Blyth and Newsham increased its voting power from

306 to 485. Nearly three-fourths of this constituency consists of working men. For the seat left vacant by the retirement of Sir George Grey at the dissolution in 1874, there were two candidates who came to the poll—Mr. Thomas Burt, the able and popular agent of the Northumberland Miners' Association, who was first in the field, and Major F. Duncan, of Woolwich. It is many years since the seat was contested, and the election was looked upon as one of the most important in the history of the constituency, and by reason of its being the first to return a veritable working man to Parliament, one of the most important in the history of the country. The election took place on the 5th of February, 1874, when Mr. Burt polled 3,332, while Major Duncan polled 585, or a majority of 2,747 for the Liberal candidate.

The election of 1874 is thus described in the *Newcastle Chronicle* :—

"The election, from beginning to end, as one of the candidates described it, was a model contest. Major Duncan and Mr. Burt were equally well received in all parts of the borough. The opposing candidates attended each others meetings, spoke from each others platforms, addressed each others supporters, and the reception accorded to both was so cordial that it was sometimes difficult to say which of the pair was the more popular candidate. As Major Duncan remarked on the election day, he and his friend Mr. Burt seemed to be a sort of political Siamese Twins. Certain it is that they appeared almost as often together as separate whenever a meeting had to be addressed. One day, Major Duncan attended a meeting at Scotland Gate. An audience of many hundreds listened patiently to all he had to say, then pelted him with questions, then held up their hands in favour of Mr. Burt, and finally passed a vote of thanks to the gallant Major for his lecture. Proof is here furnished that working men only need to be treated with respect and consideration in order to behave as well as the best in the land. If Major Duncan, instead of speaking to the miners as intelligent and orderly citizens, had indulged in the language of calumny and abuse—the contest at Morpeth would probably not have been remarkable, as it was, for the entire absence of ill-feeling. But Major Duncan learnt to respect the miners, and they in turn learnt to respect him."

The following particulars of the number of voters within the boundary of the Parliamentary borough of Morpeth, are compiled from the Register of Voters for the year 1883-84 :—In the Morpeth polling district there are 40 freemen; in Bullersgreen township the number of electors is 49; in Hepscott township, 24; in Morpeth township, 640; in Morpeth Castle, Catchburn, Stobhill, and Park Houses township, 46; in Newminster Abbey township, 28; and in Tranwell and High Church township, 8; making a total of 835. In the Bedlington polling district, or in Bedlington Parish, there are 2,409 electors. The Blyth polling district includes the townships of Cowpen and Newsham and South Blyth. The number of electors in the former is 2,085, and in the latter there are 548 electors on the roll, the total number of electors in the Blyth district being 2,633, and the total constituency includes 5,967 voters.

LOCAL BOARD OF HEALTH.

One of the principal local governing bodies, and the chief rating authority of the borough of Morpeth, is the Board of Health. The Morpeth Local Board District, as recommended in the Report of Inspector Rawlinson of the General Board of Health, London, and confirmed by Act of Parliament, was originally the entire Parliamentary Borough of Morpeth, having (in 1851) an area of 14,600 acres, and consisting of about 10,000 souls. The Board then consisted of 15 members, comprising the Mayor for the time being, 5 persons selected by the Council, 6 selected by the parish of Bedlington, and 3 by that part of the parish of Morpeth which is included in the district but is not within the corporate borough. The provisional order for the formation of the Board is dated May 26th, 1851. The election was in November of the same year. The measures and works proposed for the execution of the Board were briefly summarised as follows :

1st, A perfect system of sewers and house drains; 2nd, a full supply of pure water at high pressure; 3rd, a good surface pavement to all footwalks, passages, yards, and courts; 4th, well-formed and well-cleaned streets, footwalks, and roads ; 5th, the regular and systematic removal of all nuisances, and cleaning of streets, courts, and passages ; 6th, the regulation of slaughter-houses ; 7th, the licensing and inspection of common lodging-houses, so as to insure healthy ventilation, a prevention of undue overcrowding, and a proper separation of the sexes ; and 8th, a full and efficient system of public lighting, and all other matters and things which are set forth in the Public Health Act, or which shall be provided for in the order in Council or Provisional Order.

The area to be brought within the operations of the Public Health Act at that time included the townships of Morpeth, Newminster Abbey, Tranwell and High Church, on the west ; Morpeth Castle, and Stobhill and Catchburn townships, skirted by Netherton Moor and Hartford House aud by the river Blyth on the south; and including the districts lying between the river Wansbeck on the north and the river Blyth on the south, to the sea coast.

This order of things continued up to the year 1862, in which the Bedlington people applied for a provisional order to establish a Board for the parish of Bedlington distinct from Morpeth. This was granted, and in 1862 the Local Board of Health of Morpeth consisted of 9 members, the chairman (the mayor for the time being) and 5 members being chosen by the Town Council for the corporate part of the borough, and 3 members being appointed to represent the townships of High Church, Tranwell, Bullersgreen, Morpeth Castle, Catchburn, Stobhill, Newminster Abbey, and Hepscott, which are without the coporate borough. The clerks of the Board from the establishment have been Mr. William Woodman and Mr. Benjamin Woodman, and on the death of the latter in 1874, Mr. George Jeffrey was appointed to the office, and was succeeded by Mr. William Webb, Solicitor, who now holds the same. The sanitary condition of the borough has much improved since the establishment of the Board, but there is still room for improvement in the supply of water and in the lighting of the streets. The Board is seeking to work so as to meet the wants of the district in these and other respects.

MORPETH UNION.

The Union Workhouse is situate in Newgate Street, and is a plain but commodious building. The Union comprehends 72 parishes and townships, and embraces an area of 95,429 acres, and a population in 1881 of 36,407. The following places are comprised within the Union:—Angerton (High), Angerton (Low), Ashington and Sheepwash, Bedlington, Benridge, Bigge's Quarter, Bockenfield, Bothal

Demesne, Bullersgreen, Bullock's Hall, Cambo, Cawsey Park, Chevington (East), Chevington (West), Cockle Park, Corridge, Cresswell, Deanham, Earsdon, Earsdon Forest, Edington, Ellington, Eshot, Felton Path Foot, Fenrother, Freeholder's Quarter, Hadstone, Hartburn, Hartburn Grange, Hebron, Hepscott, Highlaws, Highlaws (High and Low) Hirst, Linmouth, Longhirst, Longshaws, Long-witton, Meldon, Middleton (North), Middleton (South), Mitford, Molesden, Morpeth, Morpeth Castle, Netherwitton, Newbiggin, Newminster Abbey, Newton Park, Newton Underwood, North Seaton, Nunriding, Old Moor, Pegswood, Pigdon, Riddell's Quarter, River Green, Spital Hill, Stanton, Thirston, Thornton (East), Thornton (West), Throphill, Todridge, Tranwell and High Church, Tritlington, Ulgham, Wallington Demesne, Whitridge, Widdrington, Witton Shields, Woodhorn, and Woodhorn Demesne. The foundation stone of the Union Workhouse was laid in 1866, and the building was opened out in 1868. It cost £4,200, and will accommodate 150 paupers. The building at the entrance above the gateway is the Board Room, behind which is the Workhouse, in which is the master's residence and rooms for the paupers. Connected with the Workhouse is an Infirmary for the afflicted, and an Infectious Ward is provided in another part of the building. The Workhouse commands an excellent view of the High Stanners and the surrounding district to the south and west. The average number in the house is about 100. The abler men break stones in the yard, and the women do the domestic work. There is to the left of the entrance a Vagrant Ward. From 60 to as far as 70 vagrants are accommodated in the course of a week. Mr. Brown has been the master of the Workhouse for 30 years, at the present and previous buildings, and has fulfilled his office with great satisfaction to the guardians. The Board of Guardians meets fortnightly, and the Rural Sanitary Authority monthly. The latter Authority consists of the Guardians for the Union, with the exception of those representing the urban districts of Morpeth, Bedlington, and Newbiggin. The Guardians are appointed annually. Mr. John Dowson is the relieving officer for the Morpeth district, and Mr. George Waterson for the Bedlington district. Mr. Thomas Waterson is the Nuisance Inspector, and there are several medical officers, chief of whom is Mr. William Clarkson.

Morpeth is situated about 291 miles from London by the Great Northern Railway, or 289 by road; and is 108 miles from Edinburgh. It is a polling place for the northern division of the county of Northumberland; it is the head of the Morpeth County Court district; is in the rural deanery of Morpeth, archdeaconry of Lindisfarne, and diocese of Northumberland. Morpeth confers the title of viscount upon the family of Howard, Earls of Carlisle.

HISTORICAL SKETCH OF THE TOWN.

LITTLE or nothing is known of the history of the town before the Saxon era. That there was a town here in the time of the Saxons is beyond doubt, for about 866 and 867 the Danish pirates Hunguor and Hubba, in their destructive progress through the county, burnt the houses of Morpeth, and slew all the inhabitants they could find. Many escaped to the woods and fells in the neighbourhood; but their huts were burnt to the ground, and everything of value pillaged by the ruthless robbers. There is very little more related of Morpeth in these early days, but it is presumed that the monks of Durham, in their flight with the body of St. Cuthbert from Jarrow, passed through Morpeth, after having rested at Bedlington. That they made no stay at Morpeth may be accounted for by the fact that the town was rising into one of some pretensions by this time, and the holy men, who not only carried the bones of the saint, but a quantity of riches, relics, and ornaments belonging to his church and shrine, were desirous of keeping in advance of the Conqueror, and finally reaching some obscure place of safety. They succeeded in their endeavour to hide themselves, and eventually they returned to Durham. There is nothing definite stated in connection with Morpeth from this period till after the Norman conquest.

On the 28th of September, 1066, William the Conqueror landed, with his army of adventurers, on the coast of Sussex; and on the 14th of October the battle of Hastings was fought, which sealed the fate of England. Nearly two years were spent in the subjection of the inhabitants of the south of England, and at the end of that time the conquering army moved northwards. York, Durham, and Newcastle were taken and destroyed, and, having left a strong garrison in each of these places, William returned to the south again. But the people of the north were not to be subdued though they might be conquered, and they rose to a man and retook Durham and York, slaying Robert de Comine, who had boastfully assumed the title of Earl of Northumberland. These risings were repeated again and again with more or less success. When news of these rebellions against his usurped authority reached the ears of William, he was hunting in the Forest of Dean, and then and there he swore that he would utterly exterminate the people of Northumberland. He again made his way to the North, and, after an obstinate resistance on the part of the Saxon defenders of York, he took the city, and spurred onward to Durham, which was also taken and fortified. The invading army then pushed forward for Northumberland, and not an inhabited town or village was left in the rear of this ruthless and destructive host. Nothing with life was allowed to remain on the land: men, women, and children, together with flocks and herds, were all indiscriminately butchered, and the cultivated lands laid waste. Famine and pestilence followed as a natural consequence of this extravagance, and such of the English as escaped with their lives from the sword sold themselves, with their wives and children, to escape a worse death by hunger. Among the many places thus destroyed was the "fair town of Morpeth," which was burned to the ground by Ives de Vescy, ene of William's captains, who carried on the work of destruction while his royal master stayed at Hexham. In this he was assisted by Robert D'Omfreville, and for their labour they were rewarded with the broad lands of their Saxon foes. Ives de Vescy had the town of Alnwick conferred upon him, and Robert D'Omfreville had Riddesdale granted to him. In the train of this man was a squire named William De Merlay. who had formerly been a servant to Geoffrey, Bishop of Constance, in Germany; but who, at the time of the invasion, joined the standard of William, to try his fortune in England. Merlay, for the services which he rendered to the cause of destruction, was rewarded with Morpeth, and a large tract of surrounding land; and he at once set himself to work to build the Castle of Morpeth,* and to repeople and rebuild the forsaken town. About two years after the Conqueror's visit to the North, Malcolm Canmore, the king of Scotland, crossed the border and marched into England to the assistance of the English against the Normans, but his services, promised so long, were given too late ; and all he did was to excite the few remaining inhabitants to a hopeless rising, and burn the huts and houses of such who refused to join him. This "friendly visit" of the old Scottish king proved very fatal to the people of Morpeth, who, having partially recovered from the effects of the invasion by the Normans, were settling down to peaceful employments again. The predatory inroad of the king of Scots exasperated William, who once more marched to the North, and this time making direct for the Scottish borders, halted at Morpeth, where he was joined by his faithful vassal, William De Merlay. The lawless soldiery of the Conqueror put to the sword all the English remaining in Morpeth.

The Normans had now been seven years in England, which by this time was thoroughly subjected. Soon after the return of the Conqueror from Scotland, where Malcolm had done homage to him, events called him over to his own domains in Normandy. With him went William De Merlay, the first baron of Morpeth, who, after fighting in Maine against Fulk, the Count of Anjou, returned with William to subdue the rebellion in England which had begun under William Fitz-Osborn, Earl of Hereford, and Ralph De Gael, Earl of Norfolk. About this time William De Merlay was married to Menialda, the daughter of Cospatric, second Earl of Dunbar, the male issue of this marriage being three sons, Ranulph, Godfrid, and Morel. Towards the end of the year 1086, William summoned all the chiefs of the army of the Conquest, the sons of those chiefs, and every one to whom he had given a fief, to meet him at Salisbury, and accordingly William De Merlay, with two of his sons and some of the men of Morpeth, set out for Salisbury plains, where were assembled all the barons and abbots of the realm, attended with men-at-arms

---

* An account of the Castle is appended to this historical sketch.

and vassals to the number of sixty thousand men. The chiefs, both lay and clerical, again took the oath of allegiance, and William, shortly after receiving these new pledges, passed over to the Continent to commence a war with France for the possession of the city of Mantes, which he claimed as his right. In the end of July he was ready to begin his war, at which time the corn was nearly ripe and the grapes hung in rich clusters. He ordered his soldiers to burn the corn and tear up the vines, and entering Mantes burned it to the ground. On riding up to view the ruin he had made, his horse swerved and threw its rider on the high pommel of the saddle, bruising him so that he never mounted again. He was carried to the monastery of St. Gervas, where he lay for six weeks, at the end of which time he summoned all his barons, and declared his will in their presence. On the 9th of September the great Conqueror expired, and his last sigh was the signal for a general flight. Among the recreant knights who left their lord on his deathbed was Merlay, who hurried home with his vassals to Morpeth.

On the death of the Conqueror, his son William, surnamed Rufus, made haste to England, and was crowned at Westminster on Sunday, the 29th of September, 1087, seventeen days after the death of the Conqueror. For the first eight years of this monarch's reign, Morpeth was left undisturbed, and this period was employed in rebuilding the houses which had so often been burnt. Morpeth at this time occupied the ground on which the Market Place and Oldgate now stands; what is now known as Newgate Street and Bridge Street being all cultivated land. William De Merlay, though extensively engaged abroad with William Rufus in his foreign wars, contrived to find time to commence the fortification of his castle, to do which he obtained a license from the king on paying a sum of money. The king claimed the exclusive right over all forests in the kingdom, which had the effect of irritating many of the Norman barons, and among these discontented chiefs was Mowbray, Earl of Northumberland, who had 280 manors. In the year 1095, Mowbray, unable longer to endure the unjust claims of the king, openly rebelled against him, which caused Rufus to march into Northumberland with a large and destructive army. Morpeth was visited by a

portion of William's army, and all the inhabitants capable
of doing duty as soldiers were pressed into the royal service. Those who refused or hesitated to accompany this
band of tyrants were immediately hung upon the nearest
tree that could be found, and their houses razed to the
ground. Mowbray, finding the king's force close upon
him, shut himself up in his castle at Bamborough, which
at that time was the strongest place in the North of England. He was eventually decoyed from his stronghold, and
carried a prisoner to Windsor Castle, where he died about
thirty years afterwards. After the subjection of Mowbray
the king marched to the south again, and the men of
Morpeth were allowed to return to their homes.

On the 2nd of August, 1100, William Rufus was slain
by a stray arrow shot by Sir Walter Tyrel while hunting
in the New Forest, and was succeeded by his brother Henry,
surnamed Beauclerk, who was crowned three days after the
death of Rufus, in Westminster Abbey. In 1129, William
De Merlay, the first baron of Morpeth, died, and was succeeded by his eldest son Ranulph or Ralph. One of the
first things done by this Ralph, after his father's burial,
was to make a journey to Durham, attended by his brothers,
and Helias, who was the clerk of St. Mary's Church, together with a large retinue of the men of Morpeth. The
object of this journey was to confirm to the monks of
Durham his father's grant of the lands of Morwick. On
the eve of Christmas day, 1137, a colony of monks from
Fountain's Abbey, in Yorkshire, in journeying through
the country, were received into Morpeth Castle by Ralph
De Merlay, who encouraged them to tarry. After having
resided in this place for a few weeks, Ralph De Merlay
offered to found a monastery for them, and gave them permission to choose a site within his domains on which to
build it. These monks were of the Cistercian order, which
was always distinguished for the beauty of the sites on
which the abbeys were erected; and when such is the fact,
it is no wonder that these old fellows pitched upon such a
charming spot as that on which

NEWMINSTER ABBEY

was built. It would scarce have been possible for them to
have selected a sweeter place in the whole county, for the

D

prospect along the valley of the Wansbeck from the abbey grounds is one of great beauty. Ralph De Merlay boasts that he himself was at the cost of building the abbey, though it is known that the men of Morpeth were compelled by him to give so many days labour in each month towards its erection. As the deed known as the foundation charta gives a fair idea of the many acres of land with which it was endowed, we will give the entire, merely modernising the language in order that it may be better understood : —

" Ranulph De Merlay to all sons of the holy church, French and English clergy, laity, presents unto them health. Know ye that I with the common consent of my wife and sons have given in free and free alms to the monks of the abbey of Newminster, which I have builded for the health of myself, of my wife, my sons, my lords, and all my friends, and for the souls of my father and mother, my forefathers and friends, and all the faithful that are dead, Rittuna and whatever belongs it in woods or open grounds and part of the wood of Witton as I set it out to them before my own people, and all the valley between Morpada and Heburn as the rivulet which is called Fulbecke runs and falls into Cottingburne and as Cottingburne runs under Prestly by a march which I made to them before my men as far as the Wenespic and thus up to the march between me and William Bertram whatever is there in wood or open land, and on the other side of the water by the brow of the hill right across to Lecha and as Lecha falls into Wdigig and by Wdigig into Meredene and by Meredene as far as the Wensepic both in wood and land. And I grant that they may have free egress for their cattle to the common pasture and my land and at Ulacam I have given to them to build their grange upon from the Eaglesnest to the Well of Erard and as the stream of that well runs into Lina and as the Lina runs as far as the march of Forum."

He likewise endowed the monastery with the woods of Witton and Ritton, which he had acquired by marriage. This house was scarcely completed before David, king of Scots, marched across the border to the assistance of Matilda, the daughter of Henry, who had been cut off from the throne by Stephen, Count of Anjou. David set himself down before Morpeth and quickly reduced it to ashes, after which he crossed the river and set fire to the abbey. The monks first prayed and then threatened; but in return were very roughly handled by the Scotch soldiery, who paid no respect to the clerical habit or the wearers. The work of destruction was carried on with such rigour that in a few hours not a stone was left standing of this house within a short year after its foundation, and the monks for a season were again left houseless.

After the destructive army of King David had departed from Morpeth, the monks of Newminster lost no time in repairing the mischief which had been done; and in order to do this the more speedily and economically, Robert, the abbot, offered free absolution to all who should assist in any way in rebuilding the monastery. There must have been a great many sinners in Morpeth even at this early date, for many were those who took advantage of the abbot's generous offer; and the work went forward so vigorously that in a very short time the monastic pile was again reared. Hodgson states that "This house fell, in 27 Hen. 8, 1535, under the act, which gave—'all monasteries to the King, which have not lands above £200, by the year.'" The possessions of the dissolved monastery were granted to various persons by Edward Sixth, and "the only sum remaining in charge to the crown, out of its revenues in 1553, was £6 13s. 4d, ; so that 18 years after its surrender, its abbot, and all its monks but one, had either been otherwise provided for, or were dead." Queen Mary, Queen Elizabeth, and James the First granted the remainder of the house and site to certain individuals, in consideration of stated sums and services. There exist' many evidences that there was a church in connection with this house, which stood on the north side of the entire establishment, and consisted of a tower, nave, transept, and chancel, about 270 feet long altogether. The cloisters were about 102 feet long from east to west, and about 80 feet wide from north to south, and were situated on the south side of the nave of the church. There were extensive buildings on every side of the establishment, especially the chapter house, and the ruins cover 320 feet from the south side of the cloisters to the north wall of the church.

To the west were gardens and orchards between the church and outer buildings, on the north side of the church was the common burial ground, and north of this was an arched gateway on the road from Morpeth to the north door of the church. All that now remains of this house is the small archway of a door of the church, which is 5 feet 7 inches wide, and 10 feet 10 inches high from the ground to the crown of the arch, though there is no doubt that it is nearly half hidden by rubbish.

The remains of this doorway is still standing, enclosed with paling, and may be seen from the Mitford road, above the Grange House Bridge, on the left.

The first bodies deposited in the new abbey were Robert and Roger, the sons of the founder, Ralph De Merlay, who were buried on the north side of the chapter house, where Ralph De Merlay in time was also laid to rest, leaving two sons, William and Roger, to perpetuate his name. The eldest of these did not long survive his father, but dying unmarried, the barony fell to Roger, generally known as Roger the first, the youngest of Ralph's four sons. This Roger married Alice, daughter of Roger de Stutteville, of Burton Agnes, in Yorkshire, the issue of which marriage was one son, Roger the second. At the death of his father in 1188, young De Merlay was a minor, and Duncan, the sixth Earl of Fife, paid 500 narks to Henry II., for the privilege of having the wardship of him, and for a license to marry him to his own daughter.

On coming of age, Roger De Merlay the second granted to the free burgesses of Morpeth all the liberties and free customs, as he himself enjoyed in his barony under grant from the king, to be held under him and his heirs. In 1194, Roger De Merlay was summoned to attend King Richard, who had just returned from the Holy Land, and who was bent on revenging himself on Philip, the French king, for the treacherous manner in which he had conducted himself towards the king of England while the latter was absent from his kingdom in the Holy Land. De Merlay, not caring to go on such a journey, sent 20 marks to the king, with a request that he might be excused from attending, which request was readily granted, as the king was more anxious to obtain money than men, of whom he had more than he could feed.

In the first year of the reign of King John, this baron paid a fine of 20 marks and "two good palfreys" for the privilege of holding a market and fair in his manor of Morpeth. Prior to this, the barony of Mitford was a place of surperior importance to Morpeth, and had long enjoyed the privileges of holding a fair and market, besides having the assize of bread and ale; but from this time Morpeth began to grow in importance, and subsequently became the market town of the neighbourhood. In 1215, Roger the second got a licence from the king to empark his woods at Witton; but the next year, appearing in arms under the standard of the rebellious barons, his castle and lands were seized by the sheriff of Northumberland, Sir Philip D'Ulcotes, nor were they restored to him till he made his peace with Henry III. The beginning of the year 1216 proved very disastrous to the town of Morpeth. For many years previous the barons in all parts of the kingdom had appeared in arms to resist the tyranny of King John, and the King, in order to subdue them, had imported large armies of foreigners to fight against his own subjects. Much of the battle and bloodshed which eventually forced the Magna Charta from King John at Runnymeade, took place in the southern and midland counties of the kingdom, and it was not till the barons of the North had given this craven-hearted king especial offence by doing homage to the King of Scots at Felton, that he condescended to visit the Borders. Shortly after the feast of Christmas, the King set out on his destructive march from Nottingham into Yorkshire, burning and slaying wherever he got an opportunity; became more savage and destructive the further he advanced and the less he was opposed. All the castles and towns that could be taken were instantly given to the flames, and the people were reminded of the raid of William the Conqueror. The foreign soldiery put the natives whom they caught to all kinds of torture to make them confess where their money was concealed. Still pillaging, burning, and slaying, this execrable host reached Morpeth on the 7th of January, 1216, and, pausing but a short time, pushed onward to Mitford, where their stay was but short. But, however short their stay was in either place, they contrived to ruin the entire district, and no house or hut was too humble to feel the fury of these murderers. The King himself set his band of ruffians the example, and in Morpeth burned with his own hands in the morning the very house which had afforded him shelter during the night. In Mitford the same was the case; indeed every hamlet on the line of march was completely erased before they had passed. Having burnt his way as far as Edinburgh, this monarch, for the first time in his destructive career, met with a show of opposition; but never being valorous except when fighting with weak men and defenceless women, he turned back and completed what, in his hurry to get to Scotland, he had left undone. Thus we find him again in Morpeth on the 25th of the same month, slaying every human being that came within reach of his sword, however young or however old. Fortunately at this time the Pope, holding a power over the King, he was afraid to touch a stone belonging to any monastic house, and thus Newminster Abbey proved to be a safe refuge for those who had fled from his lawless soldiers.

An ancient record states that the second Roger De Merlay embellished Morpeth, an opportunity for which occurred by the destruction of the town by King John's army. In 1220, with several other barons, De Merlay was summoned to march with all speed to besiege and destroy Cockermouth Castle; and in 1229, he was called upon with others to attend Alexander, King of Scotland, to meet the English king in convention at York. He died in 1239, and was buried at Newminster. In the same year, the third Roger De Merlay succeeded his father to the barony, and soon afterwards confirmed his father's grant, and also added several other rights to the burgesses, as well as granting considerable tracts of land, upon part of which historians conjecture portions of Bridge Street and Newgate Street were built at that time. In 1244, De Merlay conferred certain lands upon the monks of Newminster Abbey. He died in 1266. The barony of the De Merlays passed by marriage to William, Lord Greystock, thence to William, Lord Dacre, of Gilsland. Greystock, a descendant of whom married William Howard of Naworth Castle, Cumberland.

The latter's grandson, Charles, was created Lord Dacre of Gilsland, Viscount Morpeth, and Earl of Carlisle.

King John, after the burning of the Northumbrian castles, returned to the south, and died on the 19th of October, 1216. During the minority of Henry, in North-umberland matters were carried on peaceably and bene-ficially. In 1242, the county became a distinct part of England and under the English rule, and the year 1249 is notable for the code of laws that were then agreed upon for the administration of justice on the Border. After the death of the Scotch king Alexander in this year, and dur-ing the reign of the first three Edwards, the county was the scene of perpetual conflicts between the Scotch and Eng-lish. In 1314, the Northumbrians rebelled and appointed as chief, Gilbert De Middleton, who held possession of Mitford Castle, and Lewis De Beaumont, Bishop of Durham, was taken by Middleton a few miles south of Durham and was detained at Mitford until ransomed. Mitford and Harbottle Castles were afterwards besieged by the Scots, and the county laid waste. The next century was marked by alternate periods of peace and war, and in 1461 Percy, the Earl of Northumberland, was slain at Towton Moor, in the wars of the Roses. The various inroads into North-umberland continued until about 1500, when the Scotch were obliged to retire across the borders.

Some rejoicing took place in 1503, when the daughter of Henry VII., the Princess Margaret, was being escorted to Scotland to her marriage with James IV., King of Scot-land. Amid banquets and feasting, the princess was received into the county, and in company with the Sheriff and other gentlemen, " and many honest folks of the country to the number of two hundred, was conveyed to Morpeth, and by the town passed in fair order, where there was much people ; and so she went to the abbey (Newminster), where she was well received by the abbot and religious revested, at the gate of the church, with the cross, and after the receiving she was conveyed to her lodgings in the said place for that same night." The following day the royal procession passed on from Morpeth to Alnwick, where the princess was entertained at the castle. The royal marriage led to the union of the two kingdoms, and peace prevailed for a season, but in the reign of Henry VIII. hostilities were again renewed, and the country was invaded by the Scots. The decisive battle of Flodden, however, was a severe lesson to the Scotch, who for a time did not seek to repeat their former incursions. The county was for some time a prey to companies of marauders, and the records of Elizabeth's reign show that a number of those indicted for murder and other crimes were members of considerable families in the county, and the victims belonged to the same class. In a will made by an inhabitant of Morpeth in 1583, the testator describes himself to be dying of wounds murderously inflicted by four of the Ogle family and their accessories, in consequence of his having persumed to say that the Dacres, then lords of Morpeth, were of as good blood as the Ogles; and in a border survey of that period, it states that "the whole countrey of Northumberland is much given to riotte, specially the young gentlemen or head men, and divers also of them to theftes and other greater offences." During the reign of James the First events considerably improved in this county; the laws in force were of much effect in suppressing crime, and the people were chiefly interested in repairing their dwellings and in the cultivation of the land. From 1640 to 1647, under Charles I., Northumberland was again the scene of the battle ground for the Scotch and English armies, and in 1644 occurred the great siege of Morpeth Castle which is particularly referred to hereafter.

Concerning the history of the town from the time of the De Merlays, the records are but limited, and for the most part, with the exception of the events recorded elsewhere in the present handbook, are not of general interest. The Knights Templars, according to the Pipe Rolls, had possessions in Morpeth in 1308. Leland, who visited Morpeth about 1540, writes of the town as follows :—

Morpet, a market towne, is xii longe miles from New Castle. Wansbeke, a praty ryver, rynnithe thrwghe the syde of the town. On the hyther syde of the ryver is the principall churche of the towne On the same syde is the fayre castle stonding upon a hill, longing with the towne to the Lord Dacres of Gilsland. The towne is long & metely well buylded with low housys, the streets pavyd. It is far fayer towne than Alnwicke.

From the following document, which was sworn in Court in 1st year of the reign of William and Mary, it appears that a number of the houses in the town were destroyed by fire in 1689 :—

" Ralph Douglass, of Morpeth, in the county of Northumberland, mason, William Sadler, of the same, mason, Thomas Thompson, of the same, carpenter, Robert Donkin, Robert Mitford, and George Fenwicke, Gents., inhabitants in the same towne of Morpeth, do severally make oath, that upon Monday the twenty-ninth day of July last past, aboute two of the clock in the afternoone of the same day, a sudden and terrible fire did breake forth at the said towne of Morpeth, which by reason of the feirceness thereof within the space of three houres burnt down and consumed the dwelling-houses, kilnes, barnes, stables, and outhouses of about fifty of the said inhabitants. And that wee have seene and viewed the said dwelling-houses, kilnes, barnes, stables, and outhouses burnt by the said late fire : And severally make oath, that we judge and believe that the sum of three thousand five hundred and thirty pounds will not rebuild the same, and put the said dwelling-houses, kilnes, barnes, stables, and outhouses in good and sufficient repair, and satisfie the losse of the sevrall inhabitants."

Mr. Wm. Woodman, writing in 1849, on the occasion of an enquiry into the sanitary condition of Morpeth records that :—

One great bar to the advancement of the town, even subsequent to the union of the two crowns of England and Scotland, must have been its situation in a border county, where it was not only exposed to the continual inroads of the Scots, but to the depredations of barbarous neighbours, who, despising the arts of peace, placed their sole dependence upon plunder. Whole parishes were occupied by reputed thieves, among whom the King's writ did not run, as no legal messenger dared to venture among them. The town was without walls, and the gates, which were placed at the ends of the streets, would offer feeble barriers to such depredations.

The staple manufactures of the town were the woollen and tanning ; the former is well nigh extinct, and of the latter there are now but four tanyards remaining. The town was long known as the seat of the largest market in England for cattle and sheep, except Smithfield, all the thickly populated districts of the Tyne and Wear being supplied entirely, and the manufacturing towns of Yorkshire particularly, from it ; but this market has been almost entirely removed since 1845, when an extensive railway communication having been completed to Newcastle, all parties found it a more convenient place. A considerable quantity of stock was brought there by the steam boats from Scotland, and by the railway from the western coast. The buyers had in the railways a cheap and rapid mode of reaching Newcastle, and conveying their purchases, hence both seller and buyer naturally and properly gave that place the preference.

The most ancient part of the town is that which extends from a little below the bridge, in a straight line towards the west, until it reaches the river [Oldgate]. The street from the Market Place to the north [Newgate Street] was built in the 13th century. In the 17th century, the skeleton of the town was the same as now, and those streets and houses which are in the angle formed by Bridge Street and Newgate Street, have all been built during the present century, prior to which there was no buildings there except a number of tanyards by the side of Cotting-Burn.

The greatest prosperity of the town was from the 12th to the 16th century.

LINES WRITTEN AT MORPETH, JANUARY, 1849, BY THE LATE REV. H. K. CORNISH.

EIGHT hundred years are fled, and still the race
Of high De Merlay holds their fatherlands;
Whereon the steepy knoll the castle stands,
And Wansbeck ripples by with stealthy pace.
Eight hundred years! and saintly Robert's place,
Newminster, that upheld for centuries five
The saving Faith, long since has ceased to live,
In memory but that single arch's grace
Stands tomb-like o'er the spot, that we might know
What great and goodly relics lie below.
But better far than old baronial days
Or times monastic, are the deeds now done
By Grey and Howard, in blest wedlock one,
Who here their home of strength and piety raise.

MORPETH CASTLE.

THE CASTLE.

THE Tower or gateway of Morpeth Castle, the view of which is from a sketch drawn some years back, is conspicuous upon the elevated ground between the railway station and the town, and with the ivy-clad portions of the walls, which are still standing, constitute the remains of the ancient edifice of the De Merlays A few years ago, the gateway was considerably improved. The castle was founded by William De Merlay, shortly after the Conquest, and the walls, portions of which still remain, are of great thickness ; the masonry is rude and strong, and similar to that used in the construction of strongholds of the Norman era. In 1836, some workmen were clearing away a sand-bank near the Castle, and found a number of cannon balls, which were supposed to have been fired during the siege of the Castle by Montrose in 1644, and certain capitals of columns and ornamental stones of a Norman arch were dug up about 1830, which with others were built up in a door of the gateway. These stones were supposed to have belonged to some building, erected by De Merlay, and destroyed by the before-named siege. The gateway is considered to be the tower which was built by William Baron Greystock who died in 1359, who occasionally resided in the Castle at that time. There was no perceptible groove for a portcullis, but there were winding stairs to the top of the tower, at the corners of which were ruined turrets. Thomas Lord Dacre is known to have resided in the Castle in 1523-4, by the letters he dated therefrom. In the time of Elizabeth, Ralph Grey, Esq., of Morpeth Castle, was a county justice, and Sir Edward Grey was constable of Morpeth Castle in 1584 and 1589, and dated his will from the Castle on Jan. 10, 1627. Grose records that it seems to have been a firm stronghold up to the time of Charles the First, when it was occupied by the Scots army, who were driven from thence by the Marquis of Montrose. Some particulars of the siege of the Castle, from the Somerville memoirs are here given and will be of interest :—

Leslie, when he reached Morpeth, left a garrison in the Castle there for the purpose of deterring the king's forces, then in Newcastle, from plundering the neighbouring county, and attacking the convoys with recruits and stores coming from Scotland. Lieutenant-Colonel

Somerville was appointed Governor of the Castle, with five companies of his regiment, in all 500 men, "including the officers, with their servants—a garrison too strong, and consisting of too good soldiers for so pitiful a place," for it was "a ruinous hole, not tenable by nature, and far less by art, that if they should come to be besieged, they could not hold out two days." The ammunition left in it was only "three barrels of powder and six boxes of lead, with match conforme," and the governor victualled the place only for a month. On Tuesday, May 10, 1644, by the advice of the Marquis of Montrose, "there was presently drawn forth from the garrison of Newcastle and the adjacent field, 2,000 foot and 500 horse, besides 200 of Scots nobility and gentry, with their attendance," "to ferry out a few of their rebellious countrymen, who had rested themselves in the town and castle of Morpeth." Montrose, as general for the king in Scotland, headed the detachment, and marched as quickly and quietly from Newcastle as he could; but the rebel troops stationed in the way had notice of his approach, and both them and all the forces of the covenanters on both sides of the town never looked the enemy in the face, and many in their flight never stopped till they sheltered themselves in Berwick. Colonel Somerville, with a party of 14 horses immediately set out to view the enemy. He returned about six in the evening, and made arrangements for the defence of the Castle. Of his five companies, the third were pikemen and nearly useless in garrison service, and there was not one spare musket or halbert in the fortress. To meet this he divided his men into three companies, one to be on duty at a time and two for relief, so that the pikemen could make use of the firearms when they were relieved. About dawn on the Wednesday, Montrose began his assault, advancing 8 ensigns of foot with 24 ladders, each carried by six men to the walls. The storming was hot and furious, but the assaulters were so well played upon with shot from all quarters of the Castle, and their ladders thrown so promptly back from the walls, that after two hours' dispute they were forced to retreat with the loss of a major, 13 officers, and 40 soldiers left dead on the spot, and twice that number wounded, while the besieged lost only two sergeants, one drummer, and five soldiers, and with only a few wounded. Montrose, finding the Castle could not be won by feeble means, began to form his league within sight of the Castle, and at night they broke ground within less than half a musket shot of the walls and cast a small running trench round the Castle, both to keep them in and to serve as a breast-work to defend themselves when they fired out of it. A desperate fire was commenced next morning, which was slowly answered from within the Castle, to avoid waste of ammunition. Leslie was first informed of the siege on the Friday night, and next morning sent orders to six troops of horse and four of dragoons, nearly 800 in all, who were coming up to his army, instantly to march to its relief, and with assistance they expected to obtain on the way, he hoped they might raise the siege and bring off the garrison safely. The march was commenced, but Montrose heard of their advance, and early on the Sunday morning he struck his camp and marched against his new assailants. A detachment, which he had sent for cannon to Newcastle on the Friday, had not arrived. The besieged were unacquainted with the reasons for his sudden removal, and observed that he did not take the road for Newcastle, but quite the contrary. The governor immediately began the demolition of the breast-works and levelled the enemies' entrenchments, and what other sheds and houses were near the Castle except a great barn lately built by the lord of the manor, which he thought at too great a distance to erect any battery that could make a breach in the Castle. Montrose continued to reconnoitre and persue the detachment sent against him for five successive days, but without engagement or skirmishing; and on the fifth day after he set out, on Thursday returned to his first station before the Castle. His cannon arrived the next morning. During his absence the besieged had resolved that the garrison should be removed and the Castle blown up, which the Governor of Berwick recommended to be done; but before his advice could reach Colonel Somerville, the enemy, on the Friday morning, had blocked up the Castle, and by three in the afternoon had begun to fire upon it with six cannon from behind the great barn, which the governor could not suffer to be demolished, and which now preserved the besiegers from the shot of the Castle, most or the battlements of which in a few hours were beaten down, and the soldiers forced to leave them; many of whom were killed or wounded partly by the bullets, but mostly by the stones stricken out of the walls by the cannon shot. About twelve that night the governor determined to make a sally, in which he set fire to the barn, which was covered with rye straw, killed the captain of the enemie's guard, one cannonier, and 30 soldiers, besides wounding 50 men, and killing many horses. The governor had 13 men killed and 22 wounded. Captain McCulloch was wounded in the neck, Lieutenant Lawson in the thigh, and several other inferior officers were injured Almost all the turrets and battlements were now beaten down, but from the distance of the battery no sensible impression was made upon the walls. Montrose, therefore, on the Saturday night, caused a large breast-work to be cast up within less than 100 paces of the Castle walls, under the protection of which his soldiers worked hard during Sunday and Monday, in raising two battries, on each of which he placed three cannon; and on Tuesday " morning, by brake of day, began to batter the foir wall of the Castle betwixt the gate and the south corner of the Castle, near to some vent of the chimnies. It was Thursday, about four o'clock at night, before they had made any considerable breach, in the wall," because the cannoniers, instead of beginning at the grass and battering upwards, began very high up the wall. During a short intermission of the guns firing (for no man durst stand in the breach while they were playing), the governor had caused a deep trench to be cut betwixt the two side-walls of the Castle, directly across the breach, which he filled up with earth of the ditch, and with feather beds strongly packed together with cords—an expedient which served a good purpose while the breach was of no great widness; but the enemy, by the rising of much dust and feathers, observing with what sort of materials the besieged were defending themselves, and fearing to commence a storm across the trench, postponed his first intention until he should see what "could be done with his guns upon other parts of the Castle, which now they began to direct at random against the whole front of the Castle, whereby, in a few hours, they not only drove the soldiers of the garrison from their defences, many of them being knocked down by the shots and stones, but also in many places opened the walls so as they might have seen quite through the Castle into the open court." The garrison was now reduced to a great extremity, and the governor had received a musket ball, which entered his neckcloth, grazed his skull, and went out at the crown of his hat, " taking off some of the hide and hair of his head." The wound, though slight, bled so much that himself and those near him thought him mortally wounded, the news of which ran quickly through the Castle and terrified the soldiers, who now began to say that their governor's obstinacy had lost himself and ruined them all, in refusing to harken to a capitulation which Montrose had offered the day before. They were now forced to shelter themselves in vaults, and in the lowest apartments of the Castle, from the great and small shot poured in through the breaches, while they could only fire through a few narrow lights, opposite to each of which the marquis had placed six musketeers, who were commanded to fire as soon as they saw a musket raised to any of these loop holes. The governor now began, both by officers and men, to be charged with obstinacy in not delivering up the Castle. This startled him, and he found there was no striving against the stream, especially as two parts of his fire-arms were sprung, and the rest so furred as to be unserviceable. After some deliberation, a white flag was hung out, and some time being spent in negotiating a capitulation, the governor accepted and signed Montrose's conditions of surrender, which were that all the garrison should have their lives and liberties, that the commissioned officers and their own servants should march out with their arms, horses, and baggage, and that all the soldiers should march out with their portmanteaus on their backs and staves in their hands, and be convoyed to within two miles of Berwick. The garrison marched out at ten o'clock on the 29th of May, so that this siege lasted twenty days. Montrose lost in it one major, three captains, three lieutenants, four ensigns, and 180 soldiers, and expended 200 cannon shots. Somerville's loss was 20 men, one ensign, and two drummers.

The trenches to the west of the Castle, Hodgson writes, were probably raised by the army of Montrose. The old gateway had many dints of cannon balls in it. The shattered remains of the outer walls of the Castle show the entire extent of the ancient stronghold, the area they enclose being about 82 yards from north to south, and 53 yards from east to west. The breaches made in the walls, and the general damage effected by the siege in the interior of the Castle were never restored ; and from the remark of Somerville that it was at the beginning of the fray " but a ruinous hole," it is likely that the fortress had been neglected prior to that time. On the north side is a brook, which at one place has had a bridge across it. At the extreme end of the ridge, between the north side of the Castle and the river Wansbeck, and facing the entrance to the County Prison, is the Ha' or High Hill. In 1830, several curious stones rudely carved, and apparently having formed part of a Roman arch and pillar, were dug out of this lofty mound. It has been suggested that this high hill was raised during the siege of the Castle, and Hodgson says that " batteries may have been erected there for carrying on hostile operations against the Castle since the invention of cannon, though it is too distant to have afforded any sort of annoyance before the use of gunpowder in sieges. The remains of a cairn, or tumulous," found by Mr. Woodman, " upon it, as well as of Norman architecture, seem to carry the date of its formation into remote English antiquity," but there were not sufficient facts forthcoming to judge accurately of its origin.

THE PARISH CHURCH.

THE PARISH CHURCH, which is dedicated to St. Mary, is of the architecture of the Fourteenth century. It stands about half a mile along the Newcastle road, which branches off to the west from the turnpike between the Gaol and the Station. Hodgson states that "a former Church built on the same site has had a nave, consisting of middle and side aisles, but of narrower dimensions than the present, as appears by the first stones of an arch on each side of the east wall of the tower. The gallery at the east end was built at the cost of Mr. Edward Fenwick, formerly a scholar in Morpeth School." " Elizabeth, countess to the second earl of Carlisle, gave a sum of money to the poor of the parish, part of which was expended in erecting a gallery on the north side of the Church, the rent of which is equally applied to the poor's use, and the remaining £20 is now out at interest upon bond." " Morpeth Church is in the advowson of the Earl of

Carlisle, as the representative of its ancient patrons, the De Merlays. Anthony Beck, a proud and haughty prelate of Durham, by some usurped right, appropriated it to the chaplains officiating at his new-built chapel at Auckland, but after his death, Ralph, son of William de Greystock, recovered by law the patronage thereof. (Randall)." The Rectory, in which the Rector and Lady Elizabeth Grey reside, is on the opposite side of the road from the church, and is a substantial and pleasant residence.

With the kind permission of Mr. F. R. Wilson, F R.I.B.A., of Alnwick, we quote from his valuable work, " The Churches of Lindisfarne," the following particulars of " the Church of the Blessed Virgin, Morpeth : "—

The founders of the Parish Church of Morpeth chose a slight emi-nence about a mile southward for its site. This is now known as Kirkhill. The ruins of the castle are not far distant. The church is an ancient building of various dates. It consists of a nave with north and south aisles, and a tower at the west end ; a chancel with a north aisle ; a two-storied sacristry ; and a porch opening into the south aisle. Of these parts, the lower stages of the tower, at the west end, are the most ancient. This is transitional Norman work. The angular buttresses and groining within, and the belfry stages are of the Decorated period. In the Decorated period, the small fabric attached to the tower was removed and two arcades built where the north and south walls stood ; the chancel was also rebuilt on a larger scale, and the sacristy added. At the same time the upper stage or tower was renewed. This is the work that has been handed down to us ; but not altogether intact, for we may see that the nave was re-roofed when low-pitched roofs were the order of the day ; perhaps, a hundred and fifty years after the first high-pitched roof was reared on the new building in the 14th century. Later still, the west end of the north aisle has been renewed, and the porch built. And lastly, in our own time, a gallery and pews, inserted on the last century, has been taken out, and the building re-seated and repaired. The south arcade and aisle are considerably out of the square. There are several features in this venerable pile of special interest. Foremost, in both jams of the chancel arch are small oblique openings, technically called "squints," through which a view of the nave is obtained from the stalls. On the south side of the chancel, close upon the junction with the nave, there is a small window, transomed, on a much lower level and of a much smaller size than the three others in the same contem-porary length of walling. On the same side are three canopied sedilia, each one step lower than the other, to suit three steps placed across the chancel, where they occur. A piscina is near them ; and on the north side is an ancient aumbry. In the sacristy is a much more curious feature. This is an opening on the west side into the church ; splayed from the ground upwards to the point where it pierces the wall. The aperture is in a standing position, and on the outside of the sacristy it takes the form of a quatre-foil. There are many conjectures as to the purpose of this relique; none of which are, however, satisfactory. Some persons suggest that the chamber may have been inhabited by an anchorite, and that it was his medium of communication with the outer world, as there is no external door. Others think it possible that this hooded vent may have been formed for the safe station of a lamp or light. The north aisle appears to have once terminated at the chancel arch; and it is clear that the sacristy was finished as an external building, when the aperture must have communicated with the open air. The elongation of the aisle up to the wall of the sacristy, which was the after-thought, now encloses it in the building. My own opinion is that this opening was a chauffoir, where the priests greased their sandals. There are but few instances of Decorated work of such richness, purity and ripeness in the archdeaconry. The east window is composed of flowing quatre-foils. It has five lights. At the east end of the south aisle a three-light window is treated in the same manner.

The roof of the nave belongs to the Perpendicular period, as before indicted. It has rectangular compartments formed by intersections of timbers.

The organ is placed at the east end of the north aisle of the chancel, where a new arch has been made for it.

There is a low screen, with metal gates, at the chancel arch. The pulpit and reading desk are on the south side of it. There is an eagle lectern. Throughout the edifice, indeed, great attention is paid to elegance and correctness of detail.

The total internal length of the building is 116 feet. The width of the nave at the west end is 20 feet 6 inches: that of the east end of it is 23 feet, showing a divergence of 2 feet 6 inches. This may have been caused by an error in the setting of the north arcade. The chancel measures 49 feet by 19 feet 6 inches. The length of the nave is 58 feet. The total width across the church, including the aisles, is 46 feet.

The eastern window, of five lights, is filled with ancient glass, depicting the tree of Jesse, that has been restored. There is this inscription below it :—

"To the glory of God, in Memory of John Bolland, some time curate of this parish. His widow caused this window to be restored, and the fine old glass to be preserved, A.D. 1859."

The easternmost window on the north side of the chancel is inscribed: "George, VI. Earl of Carlisle, died Oct. 7, 1848. Georgiana Dorothy, his wife, died Aug., 1858."

The easternmost window on the south side is inscribed :—

"In memory of Thomas Sante, M.A. 26 years curate of this parish. Born 10 May, 763. Died 7th January, 1841. And of Mary his wife born May, 1762. Died 5th December, 1844."

The two light window, west of the priests' door, is in memory of Henry Brumell, obt. 29th June, 1845, and of his sons, Henry

Peareth Brumell, obt. 20th March, 1847 ; Hawdon Brumell, obt. 29th November, 1845 ; and John Brumell, obt. 21st December, 1851."

The adjoining two-light window is inscribed :—

" In Memory of Anne M. Mare, who died 29th August, 1848. This window was dedicated to God."

The small single-light, lower than the rest, is filled with glass in memory of Peter Tindale, who died May 26th, 1857, aged 89, and Elizabeth Tindale, died January 31st, 1843, aged 90.

There is a Tablet on the north wall of the sacrarium, which records that the Rev. Frederic Ekins, M.A., was thirty years rector, and died in 1842, aged 74.

On the floor of the Chancel are slabs to the memory of two children, Robert and William Midford, of Seghill, who died on the 4th and 7th of March, 1682. A Second is to the memory of William Talbot, 1697. A third, to that of Robert Bulman, of Choppington, 1738. A fourth, to that of Jane, wife of John Gekyll, 1739.

There are tablets on the walls of the aisles to the memory of members of the families of Orde, of East Orde ; Danson ; Robert Fenwick, 1693 ; and Ann Nowell, 1760.

Near the eastern end of the south aisle is a recess for a tomb, from which the effigy has disappeared. The glass of the window at the east end of this aisle is ancient. It is now [1870] in the hands of Messrs. Clayton & Bell, for restoration, as a memorial of the wife of Benjamin Woodman, Esq. At the west end of this aisle, the lintel of the window is formed of an early sculptured tomb-slab. There is also a curious recess, close to the door, at the floor level. With some difficulty I mounted the tower, and made out the inscription on one of the bells. The largest is cracked. The second reads :

CRY ALOUD REPENT. MDCXXXV.

JOHN ROBSON, PERSON, WILLIAM GREEN, ALEXANDER, FOSTER,

ROBERT SMYTHE, WILLIAM MILBORNE, WARDENS.

The smallest bears date, 1662.

There is a new lych gate at the entrance to the churchyard. The seats rise up in a step, midway, on account of the ascent in the site. An inscription along the cornices of the open-timbered roof, in encaustic tiles, reads :

" To the glory of God, and in memory of A. R. Fenwick, of Netherton, Esq., for the use of the people of Morpeth, A.D. 1861. Awake thou that sleepest and rise from the dead, and Christ shall give thee light."

The Hon. and Rev. F. R. Grey, M.A., is the Rector of Morpeth.

The churchyard is full of tombstones ; so full, that a cemetery has been formed on a beautiful rising site at the west end of it for future burials. The church walk is lined with yew trees.

The entrance to the churchyard is by a lych gate, erected in 1861. On the south side of the churchyard is a house for watchers of the dead. Occupying on eminent position in the burying ground, on the north side, is a lofty cross erected to the memory of the Rev. J. Bolland, late curate of Morpeth. The new burial ground for the parish of Morpeth was consecrated by the Lord Bishop of Manchester, July 4th, 1855.

The register dates from the year 1582. The living is a rectory of the yearly value of £1,900, in the gift of the Earl of Carlisle, and held by the Hon. & Rev. Francis Richard Grey, M.A.. of Trinity College, Cambridge.

ANCIENT CHAPEL AND CHANTRIES OF MORPETH.

FORMERLY it appears to have been a custom to build chapels at the end of bridges, for the purpose of holding services in, as well as collecting the duty which was charged for the repairing of the structures. The chapels were severally endowed with lands or rent-charges. The Chapel of All Saints stands at the Bridge-end, on the north side of the river. Before the erection of the present Grammar School, a portion of the building was used for the teaching of the pupils of that institution. It appears, from records concerning the edifice, that "in 1313 the Corporation of Morpeth, in consideration of a rent-charge granted to them, bound themselves, for the salvation of the soul of William Panetre, to find a lamp, to hang and burn in honour of our Lord and the Holy Cross, for ever, in the Chapel of All Saints, and to pay thirteen poor people on Christmas Day, one penny each for ever ! Land was granted to certain parties in 1357, in consideration that they found candles to burn before the crosses and images in this chapel; the candles to be renewed with white wax (3lbs.) at Easter and the feast of All Saints—the grantee to find at his own charge, a servant to light them. In 1380, property in Morpeth was charged with the annual payment of one taper of white wax weighing one pound, to burn before the Saviour's image, at the Chapel of All Saints." Even at that remote period, it was conceived that there was considerable efficacy in the burning of tapers and white wax candles, and the supplying of lamps, by which the salvation of the soul might be secured. Although the lands were granted on the condition that the lamps and the candles were found, and kept burning, *for ever*, it will now be a considerable period since the functions of these great lights were required, or the Christmas penny to the poor considered necessary for the absolution of Panetre! The building was for some time the property of the Corporation as trustees of the Grammar School of King Edward VI.

The Chantry of All Saints stands adjoining the Chapel of All Saints at the end of Morpeth Bridge. The Chantry was erected before the year 1300, at the same time as the old Bridge of Morpeth was built. The present foot bridge is built on the foundations and remains of the pillars of the old Bridge. John de Greystock granted a license to Richard de Morpeth to found a chantry in the chapel built in honour of All Saints. It was in the patronage of the burgesses and commonalty of Morpeth, who in 1310, appointed Adam, called the Rose of Morpeth, to conduct divine service in it, with a stipend of six marks a year. In a deed dated 1312, Adam Rose is called " keeper of the bridge and the chapel of Morpeth."

The Chantry of Our Lady, in Morpeth Chapel, was founded by Richard de Morpeth, who was appointed rector of Greystock in Cumberland in 1303, by John de Greystock, lord of Morpeth, from whom he had license to give in free alms, eight messuages and four sites of burgages of Morpeth, besides 20 acres of land, for the purpose of assigning them towards the maintenance of a chaplain, to celebrate divine services for the souls of the founder, of his father and mother, and of all the benefactors of them, and of himself and his relations, in the chapel built in honour of All Saints, near the Bridge of Morpeth. The services of this chantry were conducted in St. Mary's Porch in the Chapel of All Saints. The account of chantries dissolved by Edward the Sixth, and the foundation charter of Morpeth School, mentions only the chantries existing at that time, while the deeds in the Town's Hutch (which are still preserved, and are in the possession of the Town Clerk) mention the chantries of All Saints, of the Virgin Mary and of St. Mary Magdalene. In 1541, Sir Thomas Husband, under the common seal of the borough of Morpeth, had for the term of his life a gift of the chantry of Our Lady, or priest's service, in the chapel of Morpeth, to the intent that he should keep a school, and teach the children of the burgesses and inhabitants, grammar and other literature, as is set forth in the indenture dated February 1st, 1541. There is not the least doubt that the revenues of the dissolved chantries, in a great measure, were given to maintain the Grammar School of King Edward the Sixth.

The old chantry was partly demolished at the dissolution of the monasteries, and remained in that condition till the school was erected. At the east was a chapel which is now being converted into an Ærated Water Manufactory by Mr. Geo. Young, and the part of the chantry now remaining has been converted into two spacious shops.

EXCAVATIONS AT NEWMINSTER ABBEY, NEAR MORPETH.

Local archæologists, and some others who are interested in the architecture and arrangements of the Cistercians, have for some time been looking forward to further excavations at Newminster, in continuation of those which were begun in a tentative manner last May. Since that time subscriptions for the purpose have been collected amounting to something over £50, and Mrs. Blackett-Orde, the owner of the estate, has in the most obliging manner, granted permission to excavate, and, moreover, sent a handsome subscription towards the expenses. Permission also having been obtained from Mr. John Swan, the tenant, the ground was again broken on Monday, September 29th. A trench having been dug along the supposed line of the west front of the Chapter-house, a few courses of ashlar work were found on either side of the doorway, of which only the lower portions of the jams remain, with the bases of shafts, indicating that the arch above has been one of four orders. Portions of two skulls, and of other disturbed human bones, were found in this trench, just outside the face of the wall. An excavation begun at the east end of the Chapter-house has since extended over its entire internal area, with very interesting results. The general plan may now be made out from portions of the four walls, and of three out of the four columns which supported the groining. The north and south walls afford some indications of there having been a raised platform or dais at the east end, as at Durham. The lower part of one of the north-east buttresses may be seen in its connection with the east wall. In the centre of the east end is a stone coffin of ordinary character, apparently *in situ*, but destitute of its covering stones and slab, of its original contents, and of part of one side. It was full of earth, stones, &c., and without bones or other traces of the interment. As some of the family of De Merlay are known to have been buried in the chapter-house, this coffin may have contained one of their bodies. Portions of the beautifully moulded capital of one of the columns, including the entire moulding, have fortunately been found among the other fallen stones, and the three remaining bases are undisturbed. It seems not unlikely that this chapter-house was destroyed by removing the keystones and abutments so as to let the groining fall in, the process employed at Durham about A.D. 1797. The whole space was filled up by a mass of fallen material, among which have been noted the following objects of interest :—(1.) Key-stones of groining, with intersecting moulded ribs, but no bosses. (2.) Several cartloads of moulded stones from the ribs of the groining ; some of these retain several coats of cream-coloured wash, with indications of joints painted on in chocolate colour. (3.) Masses of fallen wall with ashlar facing, and of groining, the latter consisting of wedge-shaped stones, many loads of which have been taken out. (4.) Parts of window-heads and other worked stones. (5.) Foilated corner brackets and other springers for groining ; (no indications of " responds " or half colmns have been seen) ; the foilation is of very well marked transitional character. (6.) At the floor level a great number of pavers glazed black and yellow, and of various forms and sizes, some very small, and together indicating a pavement of eleborate geometrical design. (7.) Mortar bedding with impressions of pavers as they had been laid, distinctly showing a portion of the design. (8.) Many fragments of much decayed painted glass and of Window leading, with a little melted lead and melted glass. (9.) A hone or sharpening stone with a masons mark on it, and a piece of black " marking chalk. " (10.) An old clasp-knife, bronze mountings of book covers ? part of a hinge, iron nails, a bronze rim of a cup ? a bone pin, and other things of uncertain date ; also many bones of horses and other animals, which may have been buried by dogs. No grave slabs were found, nor were more than three or four out of the hundreds of pavers undisturbed. The grave-slabs must have been removed before the falling in of the groining, which would destroy any remains of the pavement that had been left by those who broke into the stone coffins. Only one of these has been found, but probably there have been several more, for this was the burial place of the abbots and other persons of distinction. So far as we can at present tell, the Newminster Chapter-house was a finely vaulted apartment, with internal dimensions of about 50 feet by 40, its stone groining supported by four pillars, its eastern portion raised one or more steps, and with different mouldings in its groining, its floor paved in geometrical patterns, its windows—the form of which is yet uncertain—suplied with painted glass, and its walls and groining colour-washed, and marked as a with joints by choloclate and white lines. As the chapter-house ranked next to the church in importance, its architectural features were invariably, as in this case, in keeping with the sacred uses to which it had been devoted. As the church was primarily for the direct worship of God, so the chapter-house was for the glory of God in the daily commemoration of the faithful departed, and the daily instruction and discipline of the living. Before leaving the chapter-house we may mention that as some walls and flooring of apartments on the south side of it have been found, it will be desirable to make out the connection of these with the cloister court, and also to look for the sacristy on the north side, should funds be forthcoming. While the excavation of the chapter-house was going on, another trench was dug north and south in the north transept, in the hope of finding remains of the eastern chapels, &c., and this has been intersected by others, but with no satisfactory result in the way of walls or foundations. Some flooring of thick square flags was come upon, and some foundation-stones of a wall not as yet understood. Among the earth and stones were some large plain paving tiles and a few bits of decayed glass. Quite at the north end were found portions of the tracery of a very large perpendicular window, the largest piece consists of the junction of one of the principal mullions (section 14in. by 8in.) with an embattled transom. A fragment of a subordinate mullion has a section of 10in. by 4½in. Near these fragments was found a fine moulded stone, probably part of the sill of this great window. Some oyster shells still adhered by the mortar on its upper face having been used in bedding the stone laid on it, as was often done by the old builders; at any rate joints so packed may be seen at Finchale Abbey and at Durham Castle. In the transept were found, shattered by fall of groining, &c., four early incised slabs with crosses of simple design; one has only a cross, another has also a pair of shears and the other two bear names—namely, "Joh'es de la Vale" and "Tomas," with two or three letters of an unknown surname apparently ending in "sun." Here also was found a painting. in distemper, representing a nimbed saint in a chasuble with orphrey, over a dalmatic and albe. It is executed in a rough but spirited manner, in lines of black and red, with a few touches of white, on three of the stones of a pier or pillar, which fit together, and were found lying nearly as they had fallen. The face is the best preserved part, and is full of expression. The hands, one of which might have held some distinguishing emblem, are both gone, and there is no trace of any inscription, so that it is impossible to say what saint is represented. The chasuble, without mitre, is indicative of a priest, and that is all we can say. The lines and colours are many of them so fresh that the painting can never have been exposed to the weather, thus affording an indication that this part of the building was thrown down soon after the dissolution. A stone conduit, probably for water from the roofs, was found running east and west near where the north end of the transept must have been. A small portion of the east wall of the calefactory, or common room of the monks, partly uncovered in May, has been further cleared; it is in a line with a portion of wall now to be seen abutting on the Chapter-house on the south side, and has a wall, apparently of later date, with part of a doorway, running from it eastward. It retains a bracket of transitional character, from which one of the vaulting ribs has sprung, and another bracket precisely similar was some time ago found in the garden of the Rev. W. Davey, where it now serves as the base of a cross. Indeed, there is scarcely an old building in Morpeth that does not contain "Abbey stones" as they are called, being well known to have come from the Abbey while it served, together with Morpeth Castle, as one of the chief quarries in the neighbourhood.

In looking for the east wall of the choir, which appears to have retained its original short form, as at Kirkstall, and not to have been enlarged, as at Fountains, some flooring of thick square flags was exposed with what appears to be the foundation of the high altar, measuring 13ft. 8in. by 5ft. 3in. Seven yards east of this, and probably in the outdoor cemetery east of the church, was found a rather small stone coffin containing a skeleton which had been disturbed. The covering stones were over it, but there was no slab remaining. A few feet west of it have been found remains of a tomb over a stone coffin, possibly that of St. Robert himself. The excavations must now be stopped unless more subscriptions come in. They are received by Messrs Lambton & Co., at their office in Newcastle, or any of their branch offices, or by Mr. Woodman, Stobhill, Morpeth. It is necessary to reserve a sufficient sum to cover the expense of putting the ground in order, &c. ; but should funds suffice, the Chapter-house and parts adjoining will now be well cleared out, and Mrs. Blackett Ord intends to have all excavated portions of the Abbey railed in and carefully preserved, the worked stones being kept as near as possible to the places where they have been found. The excavations are carried on under the personal direction of W. Woodman, Esq., of Morpeth ; the Rev. J. T. Fowler, of Durham ; and Mr. Middlemiss, of Morpeth, the borough surveyor. Photographs of the mural painting and of the incised slabs have been taken, and others of remarkable stones and portions of building are to be taken by Mr. Marshall, Tenter Terrace, Morpeth, of whom copies may be had

Newcastle Daily Journal, October 24*th*, 1878.

GRAMMAR SCHOOL.

THE FREE GRAMMAR SCHOOL OF KING EDWARD VI.

THE annexed engraving represents the comparatively new building, known as Morpeth Grammar School, which is very delightfully situated at Cottingwood. The foundation stone of the erection was laid on the 15th of April, 1858, by Major Brumell, then mayor of the town, the site being purchased from the Earl of Carlisle and the Corporation of Morpeth. It comprises a school room, with class room and lecture rooms adjoining, and a pleasant residence for the head-master, with accommodation for boarders.

The history of the foundation dates as far back as 1552. Prior to that time, a school was kept by Sir Thomas Husband, as mentioned above, and some part of the lands belonging the ancient chantry had been applied to the maintenance of a schoolmaster.

"On the petition of William, Lord Dacre, Greystock, and Gilsland, and the bailiffs and burgesses of Morpeth, that a grammar school might be founded in Morpeth, the king, by a charter, dated March 12th, 1552, granted that in future there should be in the town of Morpeth, a grammar school, to be called the Free Grammar School of King Edward the Sixth, for the instruction of boys and young men in grammar, and for the maintenance of the foundation he gave the two late chantries in Morpeth and the late chantry of St. Giles, in the Chapel of Netherwitton, with all the lands and rights belonging to them in Morpeth and Netherwitton, besides all the lands and other property in Ponteland, Milburn, Darreshall, High Callerton, Berwick-Hill, Little Callerton, Dinnington, or elsewhere in Northumberland, which had formerly been granted for 'the support of a presbyter in Morpeth, *a master of a school there,* or of a presbyter in Ponteland; with all reversions, rents, and renewals of leases, as amply as any incumbent of such chantries, or schoolmaster in Morpeth, enjoyed them; which messuages and lands at that time, were estimated to be worth £20 10s. 8d., a year: to be holden of the crown by the yearly payment of 10s. 8d., the bailiffs and burgesses to appoint masters at every vacancy; and, with the advice of the Bishop of Durham, to make statutes for the government of the masters and scholars, and respecting the masters' salaries, and the management of the revenues. The charter also granted the bailiffs and burgesses a special license to acquire lands, or other real property, to the value of £20 a year, as well for the support of the school, as of the Bridge of Morpeth." (Hodgson). On the 16th July, 1663, on account of the smallness of the revenues of the school of Morpeth, Charles, Earl of Carlisle, granted in trust a yearly rent-charge of £5 to the said school, out of his lands in this county. The school house had some rooms of property belonging to the foundation added to it in 1811, at which time Mr. Benjamin Woodman exerted himself considerably in renovating the establishment and restoring it to a healthy and vigerous state. The whole building was repaired in 1827, under the direction of Mr. Dobson, architect. In the latter part of the seventeenth century, Charles, third Earl of Carlisle, and William, fourth Lord Widdrington, were upon the scholars' roll. In the rebellion of 1715, these noblemen took different sides, and the friendship which they had formed at the school was highly influential in saving Lord Widdrington from the scaffold.

" In the 16th, 17th, and early part of the 18th century, the school," writes Mr. W. Woodman, " was much resorted to, and from glimpses we obtain of it during that time, we know from the number of scholars. and the eminence of the masters, that it had considerable distinction. In the early part of this century, there was but one master, who also held a curacy ; his office was a perfect sinecure, there being but a single scholar. In 1811, a gentleman, who took much interest in education, with the powerful support and ready assistance of Bishop Barrington, remodelled the school, when official classical masters, as well as French and English teachers, having been engaged, the school at once attracted attention and was attended by about 80 pupils." The management of the school continued in the hands of the bailiffs and burgesses from 1552 to 1835, when the management of the trust was transferred to seven trustees, whose names were submitted to, and approved by the Council, which had been elected according to the provisions of the Municipal Reform Act. Mr. Thos. Hopper is the only trustee living of the seven then appointed. In 1855, a fresh appointment took place, when ten names were added to the four then living. With the exception of the Mayor and Rector of Morpeth, in 1874 the number of trustees was reduced to six, and the matter was brought before the Town Council in October, 1874, by the Mayor (Alderman T. P. Cranston), who stated that certain of the trustees had lost their trusteeship by failing to attend to their duties, and as certain changes were likely to be proposed by the trustees for the future administration of the trust, he invited the attention of the Council to the matter. In July, 1875, Mr. J. G. Fitch, an assistant commissioner, attended at Morpeth and had an interview with the schoolmasters, the trustees, and the Town Council. The latter body made representations to the commissioners, and also to the authorities at London, with a view to obtain the restoration of the management into the hands of the Council. In this however, they have not been altogether successful. The charity commissioners in November, 1875, issued a draft scheme, of which the following is a brief summary : —

The draft scheme proposes that the governing body shall, when completely formed and full, consist of 13 persons. The ex-officio governors shall consist of the Mayor of Morpeth, and the member of Parliament for the Borough of Morpeth, respectively for the time being. The representative governors shall be appointed by the following electing bodies respectively in the following proportion . three by the Town Council of Morpeth, one by the justices of the peace for the county of Northumberland acting in the Petty sessional Division of Morpeth, one by the Council of the College of Physical Science at Newcastle-upon-Tyne, and one by the Board of Guardians for the Poor Law Union of Morpeth. The co-optative governors shall at first be seven instead of five, namely Sir Walter Calverley Trevelyan, Bart., Hon. & Rev. Francis Richard Grey, William Woodman, Rev. Charles Thomas Whitley, Nicholas Wright, Thomas Hopper, and George Brumell, being seven of the present trustees of the foundation. The head master shall receive a fixed yearly stipend of £150. He shall also be entitled to receive a further, or capitation payment, calculated on such a scale, uniform or graduated, as may be determined and fixed from time to time by the governors, at the rate of not less than £2, nor more than £4 a year for each boy attending the school during each school term. All boys, including boarders, except as hereinafter provided, shall pay tuition fees to be fixed from time to to time by the governors at the rate of not less than £5, nor more than £8 a year, for any boy. No boy shall be admitted into the school under the age of eight years, nor remain in the school after the age of seventeen. The examination for admission shall be graduated according to the age of the boy, and shall be regulated in other particulars from time to time by, or under the direction of, the governors. Instruction shall also be given in the school in the following subjects: Reading, writing, and arithmetic ; geography and history ; English grammar, composition, and literature ; mathematics, Latin, at least one foreign European language, natural science, drawing, and vocal music. Greek may be taught as an extra, at an additional fee of not less than £3 a year for each boy. The governors shall apply a sum of £100 yearly in maintaining scholarships of such number and value not exceeding £10 each. Of these scholarships one half shall be competed for, in the first instance, by boys who have, for three years at least, attended some public elementary school in the Parliamentary borough of Morpeth. The remainder shall be competed for by boys living in the Parliamentary borough of Morpeth, and may be awarded in favour of candidates for admission to the school, on the result of the examination for admission, or in favour of boys already attending the school, upon the reports of the examiners made on the result of the annual examination. The governors shall apply a further sum of £90 yearly in maintaining three exhibitions, each of the value of £30 yearly, tenable at one of the Universities of the United Kingdon, or the said College of Physical Science, or any place of higher education approved by them, and to be competed for by boys who are being, and have for not less than two years been educated at the school. Every scholarship and exhibition established under this scheme shall be given as the reward of merit, and shall, except as aforesaid, be freely and openly competed for, and shall be tenable only for the purposes of education.

Upon the issue of this scheme, meetings of the trustees, the Council, and the townspeople were held, by all of whom memorials were forwarded to the Charity Commissioners, embodying the views of the respective parties. The Council and the public endeavoured to secure the management being restored to the Corporation, and insisted upon the fees being kept at the figures of the existing scheme. On the 6th of May, 1876, the revised draft of the scheme reached Morpeth, but it is little other than that summarised above. So far as the governorship of the trust is concerned, one is added to the number of governors, making the governing body to consist of fourteen. The representative governors are increased from six to seven, one by the School Board for the United School District of Cowpen being the additional governor granted by the recommendation of Mr. Burt, M.P. Under the scheme, the co-optative governors are to be seven, but as they die out or resign they will, in time, be reduced to five. Mr. William

Woodman, one of that number, has recently resigned. The fees remain as in the draft scheme, from £5 to £8, per annum, the recommendations of the Town Council, and Mr. Burt in favour of their being kept at from £4 to £6, so far having been disregarded. The school has now an un-encumbered income of £600 a year, subject to scarcely any deductions for management. The head master is Mr. W. Davidson, B.A., the second master, Mr. James Kenner, B.A., and the third master, Mr. F. Lake. The present attendance at the school is upwards of 80, and the institution is progressing very satisfactorily under the conduct of the above gentlemen.

THE TOWN HALL.

THE Town Hall was built in 1714, from a design by Sir John Vanburgh. The hall was built on the site of the old Toll Booth of Morpeth, which in 1529, is mentioned as bounding on a tenement which was situated in the "Mergaitsted." An order is contained in the Northumberland session book, stating that "the old Tollbooth was going to ruin, and that it should be speedily mended, being the public meeting place for holding the sessions and keeping the County Courts." At the Christmas sessions of 1714, a presentment was made by the Grand Jury, thanking Lord Carlisle for his great kindness in erecting the stately fabric to the great convenience and satisfaction of the county, which they hoped might be improved to greater advantage. Its front was done in French rustics, and with surmounted turrets. Its interior consisted of one room on the ground floor, which had arched openings to the main street, closed with an iron gate and railing, and was sometimes used as a theatre; and two rooms above, the larger of which, till the building of the new gaol, was used as a county sessions house, and was also used as the manorial and town court-house, the guildhall for the town, and public ball-room. The smaller room contained the Town's Hutch, which is referred to hereafter. For some years, during the present century, the hall was in a state of dilapidation, but it was entirely rebuilt at the cost of the Earl of Carlisle, lord of the manor, from the plans of Mr. R. Johnson, architect, of Newcastle, and was finished in 1870. The facade is an exact reproduction of the former one. On the ground

H

floor, to the front, is a provision market, and above that is the town hall proper, which, though not a large room, has been finished in an elegant and substantial style, the fittings being of oak, and the jambs and mantel-piece of Caen stone, richly carved. There is also on the ground floor, behind the provision market, a large and commodious corn exchange, and above it on the second floor are the reading room and the library of the Mechanics' Institute. Adjoining these is the council chamber, in which the Corporation, the Local Board of Health, the Grammar School Trustees, and other public bodies, hold their meetings. The second floor is reached by a spacious staircase in which is placed a marble bust of George W. F. Howard, seventh Earl of Carlisle, and Viscount Morpeth, from the studio of Mr. Foley, subscribed for by the inhabitants of Morpeth. On the wall adjoining it are a number of ornamental brasses, engraved by Messrs. Lambert of Newcastle, which bears the following inscription :—

By the Barony of Morpeth.
[BUST].
Died 1864.
In Remembrance of George
W. F. Howard, K.G.,
VII. Earl of Carlisle,
Viscount Morpeth.

THE TOWN'S HUTCH.

The Town's Hutch is a large oaken chest with seven locks. The seven aldermen of the town, in olden times, each had the custody of one key. In this hutch, the charters, books, papers, and plate of the Corporation are preserved. Among the documents in the hutch, is an order dated 1513, made by Thomas, Lord Dacre, "that the burgesses and commonalty of Morpeth shall have a chest for the common wealth, with seven keys and locks, and the said chest should stand in the interior of the Toll-booth, and the seven aldermen each having the custody of a key." The hutch is still to the good, in the possession of Mr. F. Brumell, the present Town Clerk, and still contains some memorable documents, with very curious seals attached to some of them.

THE OLD CLOCK TOWER.

IN Oldgate Street, adjoining the Market Place, is a stone tower, containing an ancient clock and a capital peal of bells, which, in consequence of the church being at some distance from the town, are used for the ordinary parochial purposes. [A turriolum is mentioned in a deed printed under date 1310, and a turellus in 1343 ; and, in a plan of 1603, a considerable tower is drawn on the south side of Bridge Street, on the site of the old gaol]. The Bell Tower very inconveniently blocks up the entrance into Oldgate. There are six bells, which, according to an inscription upon one of them, were the gift of Major General Edmund Main to the Corporation of Morpeth. The General was M.P. for Morpeth in 1705. The tower goes by the name of the Clock House, from its containing a large old-fashioned clock. There is says Hodgson, a tradition that the clock was brought from Bothal Castle, and that it is a very old one. The lowest floor of the tower was a sort of prison or correction-house of the town, to which the bailiffs continued to commit offenders against the law till after 1800. In the records of the Corporation some interesting instances are given of the mode of punishment in vogue at the period quoted. On the 12th of October, 1741, " a Scotchman was brought before Mr. George Nicholls, one of the baillifs of the Corporation, on suspicion of picking a pockett of half a geanney and some silver, and committing other disorders, upon which the said baillifs committed the said Scotchman to the prison called the low Clock House. He then confest he had swallowed the said half geanney, whereupon he the said Scotchman was ordered to be confined for one whole week or until he voided the said half geanney, by the said baillif, and after he was so confined for four days he voided the said half geanney and no proof appearing further the said baillif dismist him after paying the constable two shillings and sixpence for their troble, by the baillif's order."— " On the 10th of June, 1743, Mary Clark, sister of Sir William Brown, taken in the publick markitt place for picking the pockitt of Jane Holmes of a geanney and a half, was brought before Mr. W. Cooper and Mr. Thomas Weatherhead, the then present baillifs ; the fact being proved against her by evidence upon oath, he committed her to the Clock House and whipted her sevearly all next day."

In 1851, W. H. Short, of Morpeth, wrote some short tales, entitled " The Watchman of the old Clock Tower," * the terms watchman having reference to the old stone figures of men which stand at the corners of the tower. At the close of Mr. Short's work, he writes as follows :—

" Still stands the age-worn old Clock Tower, overlooking the ' pleasant enough little town ' of Burns—the dream like town ' of Howitt—the birth-place of Gibson and Turner, ' stars of pre-eminent lustre ' at the period of that grand struggle for religious liberty, the reformation—where Horsley studied and wrote his 'Britannia Romana.' The adjacent, secluded and romantic scenery of the wooded vale of the Wansbeck : scenes where Akenside ' woed the tuneful nine,' and which in after years he apostrophized with such poetical warmth of feeling—which Clennel loved to survey and depict—which Raeburn has admired—and where Collingwood loved to roam, and towards which, when far away on the deep, guarding his native shores from hostile foes, his heartfelt longings were in vain directed. In modern times the learned labours of Dr. Morrison, the celebrated Chinese linguist—the literary genius of Robert Blakey, author of the ' Philosophy of Mind,' and the eloquence of one, who has made the name of Morpeth of world wide fame, all combine to show that the locality of the old Clock Tower is surrounded with a halo of interesting associations."

---

* The Watchmen of the Old Clock Tower. Price 1s. cloth.
D. F. WILSON, Morpeth.

ST. JAMES' CHURCH.

PROCEEDING now to notice the modern erections within the district, the Church of St. James the Great we consider to be one of the chief edifices that have been added to the town during the present century. The foundation stone was laid by Viscount Morpeth and his brother-in-law, the Hon. & Rev. F. R. Grey, on the 25th of July, 1844. The architect was Mr. A. Ferrey, and the erection cost upwards of £7,000. Dr. Hook, Vicar of Leeds, preached a sermon before the ceremony to a crowded audience. The church affords accommodation for 1000 persons. The windows of the edifice are filled with stained glass by Wailes of Newcastle. The church was consecrated by the Bishop of Durham, October 15th, 1846, in the presence of Lord Morpeth, nearly 50 clergymen, and a great concourse of spectators. A collation was afterwards prepared in the Town Hall, at which Lord Morpeth presided.

The Church of St. James the Great* was built in the year 1846, at a cost of about £7,000, from the designs of Benjamin Ferrey, F.S.A.

The plan is cruciform. It consists of a nave, with north and south aisles, and a porch on the north side; north and south transepts; a chancel, with north and south aisles; and an apse. There is a central tower. The south aisle of the chancel is set apart as a sacristry. There is a gallery in the south transept. The organ is placed in the north transept.

The style chosen is Norman.

Besides the entrance through the porch, there is a doorway at the west end; and a priest's door into the sacristy.

The interior † has an impressive aspect; at once rich and orderly. Among other tasteful ornamentation, it should be mentioned that the

---

* "The Churches of Lindisfarne." F. R. Wilson, F.R.I.B.A. Alnwick, 1870.

† A correct view of the Interior of St. James's Church has been published by D. F. Wilson, Bookseller, Morpeth, from a drawing by a London artist.

tympanums of the arches of the chancel aisles are filled with paintings of scripture subjects.

On a brass plate on the south wall of the south aisle is the following inscription :—

" In Memory of the Reverend John Bolland, who lived for 6 years in this town. He beautified this Church of St. James to the glory of God. He gave alms to the poor and had a kind and true heart for all men. He died in the Holy Land, April 26th, A.D. 1857. Amico Survivor S. F. Widdrington."

There are several memorials in modern stained glass. The first window in the north aisle is placed to the memory of Robert Edward Fenwick, who died 1854; the second to that of William Clark, of Morpeth, who died 1835 ; the third, to that of Francis Fenwick, of Netherton, who died 1838; and the fourth, to that of Isabella Fenwick, of Morpeth, who departed 1850.

In the east wall of the south transept, the glass is to the memory of Andrew Robert Fenwick, Esq., of Netherton, who died 1856. The window in the south wall of the same transept is in memory of George Nelson and of Mary, his wife, of Martha, their daughter, and of George and William, their sons.

The pastor of this noble new church is the Rector of Morpeth, the Hon. & Rev. F. R. Grey, M.A.

THE WALL PAINTING IN ST. JAMES' CHURCH.

These Paintings, designed by the celebrated glass painters, John R. Clayton and Alfred Bell, of 311, Regent Street, London, have been executed by two of their artists, Messrs. Hewitt and Macdonald—far the greater part being the work of Mr. Hewitt. The whole of the Painting forms one great design of which the Incarnation of the Eternal Word is, if we may so say, the key note. Thus beginning at the top of the semi-dome, there is the Dove, the symbol of the Holy Spirit, by Whose operation the Word was made Flesh : immediately below which, the Incarnate Son is represented in glory, with saints on either side.

In the next stage below, three great facts in the life of the Incarnate God are represented.

1. Jesus in the garden. Our Lord is kneeling, with the three sleeping apostles below Him, while Judas with his band appears behind, the traitor holding in his hand the bag with the price 30 marked upon it. In the sky, immediately above the " Man of Sorrows," who is their Lord and their God, is a group of angels, one of whom is presenting to Jesus " the Cup," which the Father wills Him to drink.

2. Jesus crucified. The single figure of our Lord upon the Cross, beneath which are seen, on the one side, the Blessed Virgin Mother, Mary the wife of Cleophas, Mary Magdalene and Salome; on the other the beloved disciple, Joseph of Arimathea, Nicodemus, and the Centurion.

3. Jesus risen from the dead. The risen Saviour is represented, with an angel on either side, and the smitten soldiers below.

Beneath these large subjects there is a space covered with ornamental decoration, connecting the painting above with the small subjects in the arcade below, representing the early life of Jesus, beginning on the north side with the Annunciation, and ending on the south with Christ, at the age of twelve, sitting in the midst of the Doctors. Between each of these subjects there is an angel kneeling, as ministering throughout His life to their Lord and ours, in fulfillment of the promise, " He shall give his angels charge over thee.—Ps. xci. 11.

The three central compartments represent one subject, viz., the Nativity, with the Adoration of the Magi on one side, and of the Shepherds on the other. On the north side, the subjects are the Annunciation, the visit of the Blessed Virgin to S. Elizabeth, and the birth of John the Baptist; on the south the Presentation of Christ in the Temple, the Flight into Egypt, and Christ among the Doctors.

Below this, between the marble columns, there are seventeen single figures standing—David being in the centre—immediately under the picture of the Nativity of Him who is both David's Son and David's Lord, with the legend, " I have found David My servant, with My holy oil have I annointed him."—Psalms lxxxix. 21.

On either side of David are Kings, Prophets, Priests, and Patriarchs each with an appropriate legend.

On the right side of David are Solomon and Judah, and on the left, Hezekiah and Joseph.

The prophets stand next these, Isaiah and Jeremiah on the right, and Ezekiel and Daniel on the left.

Then are next in order, the priests, on the right Aaron and Melchizedek, and on the left Moses and Joshua, the High Priest.

The patriarchs, Abraham and Isaac, are next on the right, and Job and Jacob on the left.

The painting of the dome and of the large compartment beneath the windows, are the gift of Mrs. Shields, while the single figures below the arcade are the offering of Mrs. Abbot; and the pillars of green marble are the contributions of different individuals.—From the *Morpeth Parish Magazine.*

NORTHUMBERLAND PAUPER LUNATIC ASYLUM.

THE COUNTY ASYLUM is situated at Cottingwood, about half a mile from the town, on a lofty, elevated spot, commanding an extensive view of the country around. It is a very large handsome building, in the Italian style, of red brick, with stone dressings, and was erected at a cost of about £55,000. It was designed by Henry Welsh, to accommodate 200 patients, in 1853. The minute book of the institution bears the following record of its opening:

"Northumberland Pauper Lunatic Asylum,
March 16th, 1859.

"This asylum was opened this day with 6 males and 6 females received from Bensham."

The site of the building is 210 feet above the level of the sea. The estate comprises an area of 99 acres, including the land on which the asylum is erected, and around the building are pleasure and kitchen gardens, and farming lands, some of the patients being engaged in tilling the soil, and others at the trades at which they have previously been engaged. A handsome stone chapel was erected in the grounds in 1864, to accommodate 270 persons, at a cost of £1,150. Service is conducted in it every morning, and two services on Sundays, by the chaplain, the Rev. W. J. Slacke, M.A. In accordance with the order of the committee, the new chapel was formally opened on Monday, the 12th, of September, 1864. A procession was formed from the asylum, and a full choral service was given by the Choir of the Parish Church. The sermon was preached by the Rector of the parish, the Hon. & Rev. F. R. Grey, the Chaplain, and others of the local clergy, taking part in the other portions of the service.

There are gas works connected with the establishment; and, in 1864, a brew house was completed.

In the centre of the range of beautifully laid-out buildings forming the asylum proper, facing the south, is a handsome residence for the medical superintendent (Dr. T. W. Macdowall). The apartments on the west side are devoted to the female inmates, and those on the east are occupied by the males. In 1868, new buildings were erected, providing for the accommodation of 65 males and 65 females. Two infirmaries, for males and females respectively, were added to the building, in 1872-3; and, at the present time, there is accommodation for 450 patients. Respecting the numbers within the asylum, the report of the Commissioners in Lunacy, dated the 29th of July, 1875, stated that:—

The present number of patients is 379, of whom 206 are men and 173 are women. These numbers leave 17 vacant beds on the male and 50 on the female side. Of the Northumberland patients there are 341 at a weekly charge of 12s. 3d. ; 31 out-county patients at 14s. ; and 7 private patients at 15s., 18s., and 21s. Nine months have elapsed since our last visit, and in that interval 57 men and 34 women have been admitted, 22 men and 23 women have been discharged—of whom 33 were recovered,—and 19 men and 13 women have died. The mortality has not been above the average in county asylums. There has been nothing unusual in the registered causes of death, and the institution has been free from all epidemic disorders. Seventy-one men and fifty women were dining together in No. 4 dining halls on both sides and behaved in a most orderly manner. The food consisted of pies made with Australian meet, with rice, bread, and beer, and was of good quality. The rest of the patients dine in their respective wards. We are glad to find that the number of patients attending divine service in the chapel has been materially increased since the last visit, nearly 200 of both sexes being now usually present on Sundays. The weekly dances are continued as usual, and about 58 men and 69 women go to them. The numbers reported as passing beyond the asylum estate for exercise are said to comprise 106 of the male and 95 of the female sex, a considerable increase upon the numbers who previously had this privilege. Thirty-six men work, on the land, and the total number of men employed is 122. Of the women, 33 are engaged in the laundry, and 54 in needle-work, the whole usually occupied being 127. The staff of attendants and nurses appears to be adequate ; by day there are 21 on the male side, and including 4 laundry maids, 19 for the women. There are also 2 night nurses for each side We have pleasure in recording our opinion, that many important improvements have recently been carried out at this asylum ; and, considering the short time that the institution has been in his charge, much credit is due to the superintendent for the progress which has been made.

The main entrance to the asylum is by the porter's lodge upon the highway leading from Morpeth to Longhirst. A wide macadamised roadway, with well-formed hedges on each side, well lighted at night time by lamps, ascends in a winding manner to the height on which the asylum is erected. There are footpaths in various directions through the woods and grounds, affording opportunities for the patients taking exercise. The grounds surrounding the building are exceedingly well laid out with trees, shrub-beries, and flower beds. Having personally visited the institution, we had the advantage of obtaining a variety of information on the spot from one of the officials. Although an asylum must at all times be associated with depressing ideas, the general impression of our visit was very satis-factory, as we could see how carefully the inmates are

I

attended to, and how anxious the magistrates and officers are to make the place as comfortable as possible for the afflicted sufferers. The manner in which the chief female wards were furnished and painted was really surprising. The walls were painted various tints, and were hung with a number of excellent engravings and oleographs. A variety of plaster images added to the adornment of the appartments. Several specimens of cage-birds, in neatly constructed cages, were exhibited on the tables, and sent forth a cheerful chorus of song in what appeared a most cheerful place to an ordinary observer. The colours of the paint on the wall, and the hangings of the windows, were bright and cheerful, and were well calculated to remove all dull, morose, and unnatural feelings of the mind to a state of lively, spirited, and sensible vigour. When we entered many of the women were busily preparing for tea; others were sitting quiet, patiently examining the pictures of an illustrated London paper, and children's magazines with interesting wood cuts facing every page. Everything was remarkably clean about the long room, and the females appeared to be very tidy. But their faces told the tale of their need of a dwelling removed from the houses of their friends and the general populace. One woman endeavoured to obtain hold of my hand, and whispered in my ear, " Could you not get me out of here?" This was followed by a number of assertions which indicated too plainly that the patient was not fit to be " out " of there, and made one feel glad there was such a habitation for the insane. One's heart might have been turned at the sight of a beautiful little girl patient, seven years of age. She was particularly addicted to running upon the railways between the rails, and could not be safely permitted from an asylum. We followed into some spacious rooms, the floors covered with carpets; the valances and table covers were beautiful, and the dresses worn by the women were of great variety of colour and trimming. A finely lighted room, most comfortably and cheerfully furnished, introduced to our view the infirmary of the asylum. There were several special chairs and conveniences for the sick. Antimacassars of various colours hang over the chair backs in gay profusion, and I was told were all the work of the patients. The bedding, wash stands, basins, mahogany-fitted bath, and every thing connected with the infirmary ward were scrupulously clean, and the decorations corresponded with those of the adjoining wards. The general arrangements of the wards showed fully that the superin-tendent fully endorsed the recommendations of the Com-missioners, made in the time of his predecessor, Mr. Richard Wilson, when they suggested, as respects the personal condition of the patients, the adoption of a greater variety in colour and material of their dress, and the disuse of the gray cloth then worn by many, which showed too much of a prison or workhouse character. After leav-ing the rooms where the females were commencing with tea, and passing through the infirmary ward. we had a rapid glance within the chapel, which is elegantly fitted up. Re-turning to the asylum, we passed to the upper storey of the building, in which are the bedrooms. They were also quite clean and of comfortable appearance. A nurse sits up all night in the room and is ready to attend in case of any thing going wrong. There are also two nurses at hand in the event of assistance being required by the nurse in attendance. We next visited the dining room of the male patients. The bread put before them was really good. One poor fellow addressing us, said, "It is the Lord's Supper." The male side of the building is a counterpart of the female side, and equally attractive in the way of interior adornment. At the back of the building are the laundries, the drying closets, visitors to patients rooms, the bakehouse, large and numerous work-rooms for shoe-makers, joiners, blacksmiths, tailors, upholsterers, mat-makers, &c., &c There is also a deadhouse, and medical officers' room attached. There is a brewery, where the patients help the brewer to brew the beer, which forms part of the liberal diet afforded the inmates. There are green-houses, summer-houses, airing courts, recreation rooms, bath rooms, gardener's house, gardens, vineries, plants, and beautiful grasses and ferns, which all add to the appearance of the asylum, and employ much of the time of some of the patients.

Concerning the various means employed for the recovery of those placed here for treatment, Dr. Macdowall, reports as follows :—

Medical treatment, the value of which is becoming more and more recognised, has been assiduously pursued in suitable cases. Being at the same time convinced of the great importance of systematic occupation, exercise, and amusement, I have devoted to these departments of treatment constant attention. In addition to the usual daily exercise in the airing courts and grounds, large parties of both sexes walk in the country every Saturday afternoon. These excursions are greatly enjoyed by the patients. At present, the number of each sex joining these excursions is about 60. During the summer, three pic-nic parties went by rail to Newbiggin. On each occasion about 60 patients formed the party. To the indoor recreations considerable additions have been made. Besides the usual weekly dance on Wednesdays, the amusement hall is filled every Monday night, when a programme of vocal and instrumental music is gone through. In order that the musical talent of those connected with this asylum may be developed and made available when occasion may require, I have a weekly class at which church music is practised. In an asylum, any systematic exercise which engages the attention and promotes discipline, tends to exert a beneficial effect upon the patients. Considerable additions have been made to the library. By the diligent circulation of books from ward to ward, the utmost is made of what we possess. Daily, weekly, and illustrated papers, and monthly magazines, are freely circulated in the wards.

THE MASONIC HALL.

The foundation stone of the Masonic Hall was laid by the Mayor of the borough, Ald. T. P. Cranston, on Friday, October 23rd, 1874. The site of the building is in Copper Chare, which is a short distance from the centre of the town, and is easily accessible from Newgate Street. The ground occupied is 66 feet long and 50 feet in width. The hall consists of a large room for public meetings. &c , on each of two storeys, measuring 63 by 29 feet inside; hall keeper's room and offices, ante-rooms, cloak-room, &c. The proceedings of the foundation stone laying were commenced by Mr. W. Davidson, B.A., who said that all assembled would acknowledge the importance of the occasion on which they had met, not only to the Freemasons, but to the inhabitants of the borough, as it was admitted on all hands how great was the need for a large public hall adapted for various purposes. The Mayor, having laid the stone with the assistance of Mr. Middlemiss, declared the same to be well and truly laid. He expressed his pleasure in taking part in that ceremony, and his decided conviction that such a building was needed in the town. Although the building was promoted by the Freemasons, it had been thought well to have it enrolled as a Limited Liability Company, and the public had every opportunity of taking shares in the Company. Mr. D. F Wilson and Mr. Thos. Cranston delivered addresses, and moved a vote of thanks to the Mayor and the Town Council for their presence, which was carried with acclamation. This concluded the ceremony. The building was completed in 1875, and has since been used for various purposes, and is in constant demand.

THE ROMAN CATHOLIC CHURCH.

THE Roman Catholic Church, dedicated to St. Robert (the first abbot of Newminster), in Oldgate Street, is a stone building of the early English style, having a well-proportioned square tower and spire, at the west. It was built in 1849, at a cost of £2,400, from designs by Mr. T. Gibson, Newcastle, and the height of the spire is 115 feet. It was opened for divine service by the Right Rev. Dr. Hogarth, vicar apostolic, on the 1st of August, 1850. The interior has a very beautiful appearance; most of the windows are embellished with richly-stained glass. The Rev. Father Wm. Davey is the priest. The school adjoins the church, and there is also a substantial residence for the priest in Oldgate Street, adjoining the church grounds. The house is said to be that in which Lord Collingwood resided when he lived in Morpeth. On the opposite side of the street are the Collingwood Gardens. In the churchyard, near the edifice, a monument is erected to the memory of the last priest of the church, the Rev. Father Lowe, who was highly esteemed by his congregation, and held in great respect by all classes of the community in the town. Hodgson records that, while Parliamentary restrictions forbade Roman Catholics to hold public worship in this country, persons in this neighbourhood of that communion assembled secretly for that purpose in a house in Bowlesgreen, where mass was said once a week by a priest from Longhorsley. They had, after this, a chapel in Oldgate, which was built in 1778. The first minister was the Rev.

Mr. Turner, who officiated until 1802, when he was succeeded by the Rev. H. Lawson, who died in 1829, and was
buried in Morpeth Churchyard, where a stone is erected to
his memory. The Rev. C. Shann was the next priest.

THE PRESBYTERIAN CHURCH

St. George's English Presbyterian Church is pleasantly
situated at the north-east end of the New Bridge, and was
erected on the site of the ancient Mill of Morpeth.* The
foundation stone of the church was laid by R. Barber,
Esq., of Manchester, and the edifice was built in 1861, at
a cost of about £4,000. The opening sermons were preached by Dr. Guthrie, of Edinburgh, and Dr. Hamilton, of
London. The congregation is by far the most considerable
in numbers attending the Nonconformist churches of the
town. The church is a handsome structure, with a tower
and spire. The clock of the tower has three dials facing
the west and the north and south. The clock answers the
purpose of a town-clock, and is lighted with gas at nights,
partly at the expense of the town. On the dials are the
words, " Redeem the time." The minister of the church
is the Rev. A. H. Drysdale, M.A. In connection with
the church, are Mission-stations at Pegswood, Fenrother,
Newton Underwood; and, at Spring Gardens, in the district of Bullersgreen, services at the latter being conducted
by the Rev. Dr. Robinson. The sabbath school meets in
the school room, Cottingwood Lane, and is superintended
by Mr. J. Hann. A day school is also taught in the same
place by Mr. James Fergusson, at which there is an average
attendance of 162. The church-officers are :—Session
clerk, Mr. J. Hann, ; clerk of deacon's court, Mr. W. J.
Atkinson ; treasurer, Mr. J. Hann ; church-officer, Mr.
John Mackay.

---

* The burgesses of Morpeth bound themselves and their heirs in
1212, not to grind the corn which grew upon the land which they
farmed of William, son of Thomas de Greystock, anywhere but at
the Mill of Morpeth.

The last report presented to the congregation, on **May** 15th, 1883, states that the real property belonging to the congregation, consisting of the church, the manse, and the school, is entirely free of debt and in good repair, and may be fairly estimated in value at £7,000. Insurances have been effected on the buildings to the amount of £4,150. The personal or monied property consists of :—Invested in consols, £176 1s. 3d. ; in the hands of the treasurer, bearing interest, £82 13s. 0d. ; total, £258 14s. 3d. The deeds and securities of the real and personal property are in the hands of the treasurer, as custodian of the same. There is also £100, the Jubilee gift of the late Dr. Anderson, for nearly 40 years minister of the church, invested in Russian bonds, for the benefit of the poor of the congregation, yielding an annual return of £5 12s., which is distributed among the poor at Christmas. The deed of purchase is in the hands of Mr. W. J. Atkinson, clerk of deacon's court, who was appointed by the court curator of the same.

Hodgson (Morpeth : p. 77, 1832) states that :—The Presbyterians had no fixed meeting-house here before the year 1721. For some time before that year, they are said to have assembled in a house on Cottingburn, where Mr. Railston's tan-yard now is, and a little above their present house, which, according to its title deeds, stands on ground which had belonged to Newminster abbey. The indenture which confers the property on the foundation is dated July 20, 1721 ; and is between Wm. Crawford in the first part ; Sir William Middleton, bart. ; John Cay, of South Shields, esq. ; Reynolds Hall, of Newbiggin ; Cumberland Leach, of Belsay ; Benjamin Bennet, of Newcastle ; Jonathan Harley (Harle), of Alnwick, M.D. ; and John Horsley, of Widdrington, gent., on the other part ; and among other things sets forth, that in consideration of £10, the premises were demised on a determination term of 999 years, which commenced 20 Sep. 27 Ch. II., to the said parties of the second part, upon trust that they should permit a chapel or meeting-house to be erected thereon, if the laws of the realm would permit, connive at, tolerate, allow, or indulge the same to be used or employed for and as a meeting-house, and as an assembly of a particular church or congregation of protestants dissenting from the church of England for the exercise of their divine and religious worship therein, the minister to be a protestant, able minister, who in judgement and practice as to church discipline and government should be a presbyterian, and not of any other persuasion, and should be orthodox and sound in the faith of our Lord Jesus Christ, and profess the doctrinal articles of the church of England, and be qualified according to the statute of the first of William and Mary.

At the death of George Atkin, elected minister of the Presbyterian church in 1817, Matthew Brown stood a contest for the position, with Thomas Wood, and was chosen by a small majority of the congregation. This contest caused a schism, the minority of which built the Independent Chapel and chose Mr. Wood for their minister; he, however, did not receive ordination on the occasion, but left Morpeth in 1830.

THE FOLLOWING IS A MEMORIAL MINUTE OF THE SYNOD OF THE PRESBYTERIAN CHURCH OF ENGLAND IN REFERENCE TO THE LATE

REV. JAMES ANDERSON, D.D.,

Minister of St. George's Church, Morpeth, for nearly 40 years : —

" THE SYNOD records with deep and tender sorrow the death of one who was conspicuously its father, the REV. DR. JAMES ANDERSON, of Morpeth.

" His name, presence, and character were bound up with its whole course for nearly forty years—from 1843 to 1882, the year of his departure.

" One of the brave men of the Scottish Disruption of 1843, he threw himself, with all his unworn and manly ardour, into the early difficulties of the Presbyterian Church in England, especially in the North, where it was utterly disorganised and disheartened; and he did it most signal service as a wise administrator, an undaunted pioneer, and a large-hearted initiator and promoter of every good cause.

"To the College, in its days of weakness, he was an unfailing friend; and out of his Jubilee Testimonial in 1872 he generously endowed the Scholarship which bears his honoured name : to the education of the young of the Church he was passionately loyal; and of the Union that formed the Presbyterian Church of England, he was a firm and unhesitating supporter. And when the Union took place, all at once turned to him as first Moderator, none being equal to him, or even second, through length of service, and through that influence, veneration, and love which a certain high and uneque individuality gave him. And ever since his presence among his brethren has gladdened, while it solemnised them, as their sympathy with his growing weakness of body only deepened their sense of his growing strength of fatherly affection to all, and of his manifest increase of childlike trust in God and communion with his Master and Saviour.

" Many as are the Memorials of the fruit of his work, 'even unto old age,' it is the man himself that is his best memorial, now that he is gone.

" His very stature, soldiery and commanding, even when bending under the weight of more than fourscore years; his rapid, vehement, yet curiously measured, speech, with its antique, classical tincture; his look, keen with sagacity, keener with integrity, keenest of all with love to God and his fellows; his continued freshness of spirit and youthful interest in new and progressive views on social and ecclesiastical questions; his fearless and unsparing advocacy of the cause he espoused, that, in its perfect honesty, left no trace of bitterness; his flashes of humour and of indignation, that only threw out his habitual devoutness into finer and more genial attractiveness—all these, and more, drew to him reverence as to a father and loyalty as to a chief.

"Never shall the Synod forget his chivalrous sense of honour, his child-like unconsciousness of self; the manly courage with which he clung to the cause his judgement and conscience approved ; the manly sagacity and impetuosity with which he mastered details and moved men ; and, above all, the ever increasing saintliness of look and bearing—image of the good man God had made him—in which there was no exclusiveness of asceticism and no relaxation of spirituality.

"And now the old man is not 'yet alive,' and the prophet is taken from its head ; and the Synod, as it stands around, looks down upon his grave with filial sorrow, and looks up, whither he himself has gone, with pathetic joy. But such men never die, and never depart from the Church and the world they blessed. This broken, formal record is only one of the records of yearning sorrow and grateful affection that will abide long in many hearts, and that will ever and again come up in them a cheer, a hope, an inspiration to live in and for Christ, in their own place and in their own day, a life as rich as his was in true human love and in humble Divine trust.

"The Synod further directs that this Minute be sent as a faint token of its tender sympathy with his family, who miss and mourn him daily; and with his congregation, among whom he was indeed a father and a man of God."

THE CONGREGATIONAL CHURCH.

THE foundation stone of the Congregational Church was laid in King Street, on the 5th of March, 1829, and on Sunday, the 15th, sermons were delivered by the Rev. T. Wood. A.B., on the principles of congregational dissent. Viscount Morpeth, M.P., and William Ord. Esq., M.P., each presented £5 towards the erection. The church was opened on the 20th of September, 1829.

"The Congregational Church at Morpeth was formed in the year 1831, under the pastorate of the Rev. W. Froggatt. The chapel was erected and the congregation gathered a year before. The Rev. George Atkin, the minister of the Presbyterian Church being in friendly intercourse with the Congregational ministers of Newcastle, North Shields, and Sunderland, and often inviting them to his pulpit, some of the most active of his people acquired a taste for their ministrations, and on his death, about the close of the year 1829, measures were taken for obtaining a minister of the Congregational order, the constitution of the Presbyterian Church being understood to be such that a Congregationalist might conscientiously became its minister. The friends of this faith, not succeeding in their endeavours now seceded, and built the present commodious chapel. Their efforts to form a new congregation were greatly favoured by the popular talents of a young minister, and the chapel was opened under the most flattering auspices. A misunderstanding, however, arising between him and them, he suddenly left, and at the close of the year, the Rev. W. Froggatt was invited to supply the vacant pulpit, and the church grew, and enjoyed uncommon harmony, during the seventeen years of Mr. Froggatt's pastorate. In 1818, the Rev. Wm. Ayre became minister of the church, and remained in that position until the beginning of 1872, when ill-health and old age compelled him to resign. He still, however, resides in the town, and with comparative rest he has recovered some of his former vigour, so that the churches of the district enjoy his occasional services.*

In the spring of 1872, great improvements were made in the place of worship, so far as the interior was concerned, and in May of the same year the Rev. David Young, B.A., became minister of the church. Twelve months later an organ was added, which has been a great help to divine service. It is very much regretted, however, that the place of worship occupies such a bad position. It is situated in King Street, one of the worst districts of the town. [The entrance is from the Back-way, which is reached by Bell's Yard from the front, and Union Street from the back part of the town]. The front abuts on a dilapidated block of houses, utterly unfit for the residence of human beings. A brewery, two slaughter-houses, and a tallow candle manufactory are in immediate proximity. One of the worst nuisances to the congregation arises from the animals which are kept in the adjacent buildings. Very frequently, indeed, are the services disturbed by an irregular chorus of donkeys and dogs.—Abridged from a paper by the Rev. D. Young, B.A., in the *Northern Light.*

THE WESLEYAN METHODIST CHAPEL.

In connection with the Wesleyan cause in this town, it may be mentioned that the Rev. John Wesley often preached in Morpeth, between 1748 and 1790. On the 18th July, 1748, Mr. Wesley records in his journal, he began his journey northward,, having appointed to preach in Morpeth at noon. "As soon as I had sung a few verses at the Cross," writes Mr. Wesley, "a young man appeared at the head of his troop, and told me plainly and roughly, 'you shall not preach there.' I went on; upon which he gave the signal to his companions, who prepared to force me into better manners; but they quickly fell out among themselves. Meanwhile I began my sermon, and went on without any considerable interruption; the congregation softening more and more, till, toward the close, the far greater part appeared exceeding serious and attentive." Mr. Wesley preached again at the Market Cross on the 8th of August, 1748, and on the 6th of September, 1749, when he spoke at one side of the Market Place. "It was feared the market would draw the people from the sermon; but it was just the contrary; they quitted their stalls and

---

* Since the above was written Mr. Ayre has joined the great majority.

there was no buying or selling till the sermon was concluded." Writing on the 13th of June, 1757, Mr. Wesley states that he " preached the love of Christ to sinners in the Market Place at Morpeth. Thence we rode to Placey (Plessey). The society of colliers here may be a pattern to all the societies in England. No person ever misses his band or class : they have no jar of any kind among them; but with one heart and one mind, ' provoke one another to love and to good works.' " At noon, on the 27th of May, 1780, Mr. Wesley preached in the Town Hall, and at their own preaching-house, in May, 1784, and also addressed large congregations in the open-air at subsequent seasons in the Market Place.

The preaching-house above referred to was a School Room in Well Way, where the services were held until 1809. In this year the Wesleyan Methodists purchased a chapel in what was then called Manchester Lane. This building was erected by the Countess of Huntingdon. Fourteen years afterwards the greater part of this chapel was re-built. It remained in use for sixty years, and on May 21st, 1883, the demolition of it together with a cottage at the rear or north of it commenced. During the process of pulling down these buildings search was made for a foundation stone with its customary contents ; but none was found, and from that source no history of the building and its predecessor could be obtained. On the site thus enlarged a very handsome Chapel has been erected. The front is built of the best stone which the district can produce, viz. :—that from Nunriding Quarries. Its architectural appearance is chaste and attractive. In style it is the same as that which prevailed in the 15th century. The principal feature of the front elevation is a lofty central gable containing a large traceried window of five lights and surmounting two deeply moulded and recessed arched doorways. On either side of the central gable and divided therefrom by buttresses are lower wing walls pierced by two tiers of traceried windows. All the windows of the chapel are of tinted Cathedral glass glazed in lead in lozenge-shaped pieces. The internal fittings are made of pitch pine and have been very much admired. The sitting accommodation provided is for 360 persons or 110 more than its predecessor. Underneath the chapel there is a school, a vestry, and heating chamber. The former has accommodation for 120 scholars, and the whole of these apartments are on a level with the ground at the rear of the building, which is lower than that at the front. The chapel was opened on April 1st, 1884, by the Rev. Richard Roberts of London, who preached from the text, Revelations, Chap. I, Verses 12 & 13. The entire cost of the building was £1,620 of which £190 remained to be raised at the close of the first day's services. The mayor and corporation, accompanied by their mace-bearer, with that emblem draped in black, as a token of mourning for the Duke of Albany's death attended the service.

Wesleyan Methodism has never stood to the front numerically in Morpeth itself, yet from it have sprung a number of societies; and the Blyth circuit. At present Morpeth is the centre of a circuit comprising besides itself, Guide Post, Scotland Gate, Ashington, Pegswood, and Netherton. The number of enrolled members in this circuit is about 160, and nearly 1,000 people assemble every sabbath to listen to the ministrations of the lay and ordained ministers who carry on its work. The residence of the minister, who usually stays three years, is 17, Howard Terrace.

THE PRIMITIVE METHODIST CHAPEL.

The Primitive Methodist Chapel, situated in Manchester Street, is a very neat and comfortable structure, capable of holding about 200 persons. This energetic denomination has long played a very prominent part in ministering to the spiritual wants of the mining population in the vicinity, but it is only within the last few years that they have taken a position in the town of Morpeth. The chapel was built in 1871, and forms at present part of the Blyth Circuit; but from the rapid extension of the collieries of the neighdourhood of the town, and the consequent enlargement of the Blyth Circuit, it is anticipated that ere long, Morpeth and the adjacent villages will be constituted an independent Circuit.

RAILWAY STATIONS.

MORPETH Station is the first of importance upon the North-Eastern Railway, after leaving Newcastle, on the main line to the north. The ordinary express trains stop at Morpeth, and the trains to and from Reedsmouth and Rothbury run upon the Wansbeck Valley line (North British), to meet the fast trains, north and south, in the morning, at mid-day, and in the evening. Passenger trains for the Wansbeck Valley line start from Morpeth Station. The Blyth and Tyne Railway runs to the east from Newcastle to Backworth junction, thence north by the coast to Morpeth, where it has a terminus. The present station on the main line has been very much enlarged and improved, and the Blyth and Wansbeck trains run right into it. There is also a Booking Station on the north side for Passengers going to Rothbury and the North. Passengers ariving at the south side instead of crossing the rails as formerly, pass under the line through a tunnel, which makes it nearer and safer, and the footpath has been cemented and much improved, making the entrance to the town pleasant and agreeable in wet weather.

The portion of the North-Eastern Railway between Newcastle and Berwick, extending from Newcastle to Morpeth, was opened for passenger traffic on the 1st of March, 1847. The line from Newcastle to Berwick throughout was opened on the 1st of July, 1847, when a train of carriages left Newcastle and reached Tweedmouth in about three hours. On the 5th of July, of the same year, the mail coach between Edinburgh and Newcastle, which had been established for 61 years, reached Newcastle for the last time.

The Morpeth branch of the Blyth and Tyne Railway was completed, and the last rail laid, on the 25th of May, 1857.

The Wansbeck Valley line runs to Reedsmouth, where it joins the Waverly route of the North-British Railway.

By a branch from Scots' Gap junction, the line runs to Rothbury, where it terminates. There is only a single line of rails on the route. The line to Scots' Gap was opened in 1862 by the Northumberland Central Railway Company, who afterwards sold it to the North-British Company. It was intended to carry the line through the centre of the county by Wooler and Cornhill, and form a junction there with the North-Eastern Railway, but the project has not been proceeded with.

THE BRIDGES.

MORPETH BRIDGE, which crossed the Wansbeck where the wooden foot bridge, known as the Mayor's Bridge, is now erected, was a strong ancient structure, with two wide arches. It was narrow and exceedingly steep. Before the present stone bridge was erected, the mail coaches had to cross by it, and it was very inconvenient and dangerous. Two of the mail coaches, about 60 years ago, carried away the battlements of the bridge, and were thrown with their passengers and horses into the river, in one instance fatally. Prior to the dissolution of chantries, the repairing of the structure lay upon the keeper of the Chapel and Bridge of Morpeth, probably according to some arrangement with the Corporation. After that time, Edward the Sixth, in consideration of revenues granted to them for that purpose, imposed the burden of not only maintaining two masters in the Grammar School, but of " the maintenance of and annual repair of a certain stone-bridge, commonly called Morpeth-brigge," upon the bailiffs and burgesses of the town. On the 13th February, 1832, at noon, the old bridge was closed except for foot passengers. The old fabric has since been blown up, and an iron and wood foot bridge erected on the piers of the ancient pile. In the centre of the new foot bridge are tablets inscribed as follows :— " Erected by Public Subscription, 1869. Joseph Jobling, Mayor. Swinney Brothers, Morpeth."

The new substantial bridge, at the entrance to Morpeth, was built in 1831. The Act of Parliament for its erection received the royal assent on the 1st of June, 1829. The site chosen by Mr. Telford is about 30 yards below the old one, and the designs of the bridge were by Mr. Dobson, architect, of Newcastle. The bridge consists of three arches, the middle one of 50 feet, and the two side ones of 40 feet span ; the breadth of the arches across their soffits is 32 feet 6 inches, the largest rising 10 feet, and the other two 13 feet each. On the 13th of February, 1832, the new bridge was opened for the use of the public on payment of toll. On the 4th September, 1848, the toll was discontinued, the entire cost of the erection, £9,500, with interest, having been paid off.

The foundation stone of a Suspension Bridge, for foot passengers, across the river, at the west end of Oldgate, was laid on the 20th November, 1826. The bridge was built by subscription, and opened in 1827. This structure has also been replaced by a wood and iron bridge similar to that lower down the river.

A substantial bridge at Morpeth Grange Ford was built in 1836, by subscription.

The High Ford Bridge, near Mitford, was built in 1829, and 1830, the foundation stone being laid by B. Mitford, Esq. The cost of the erection was defrayed by subscription.

A Foot Bridge has been recently erected at the end of the High Stanners for the accommodation of those living at Bullersgreen, for which the public are much indebted to Mr. Sanderson, the worthy Town Inspector, it being got up chiefly through his instrumentality.

BOUNDARIES.

THE Boundaries of the borough are set forth as follows, in a memorandum, dated April 3rd, 1758, on the occasion of the grand jury walking the bounds :—" Down the Walk-mill-close and along the Slidden-heugh and crossed the water at the East Mill Warren-head and into the Farcey-holes, and thence into the Parish Haugh and along by the north hedge of the Haugh, then along part of the Parish Haugh Lane, and in at the Miller's Grey Hook, and along the west hedge of the said close, and along God's Ridge-head closes, and into the Gleedy heugh and then crossed the turnpike at the low grates and through the close leading to Jerry's banks, and along the foot of the High hill, and into the castle wood, and along by Watty's hole, and so into the standers and through the garden in the same, walked over the water called Bowlsgreen-steps to the bounder stones set to ascertain Morpeth bounder, and from Beggar-road down to Cottingwood-lane along Well-close to the place where it was begun."

STREETS.

BRIDGE STREET was formerly known as Briggate or Brig-street, and extends from the Market place eastward to the bridge at the south entrance to the town. Some of the houses in it are referred to in documents bearing date 1465, 1526, &c.

Newgate Street runs from the Market place to the north end of the town, where Bullersgreen is situated. Newgate is mentioned in the records of the town, 1361-64. It has been conjectured that it was built in the North Field, about the time that the town obtained a charter for a market. It had a place in it called a Lowe, a tenement upon which in 1376, paid half a stone of wax yearly to the keeper of the Chantry of All Saints in Morpeth.

Oldgate Streets extends from the Market place westward to the foot bridge over the river. The Dispensary, when established in 1817, was situated in Oldgate. In 1546, on the north side of the street, there was property belonging the Abbot of Newminster. In 1559, the Corporation of Morpeth, who have still property in the street, let a house on the north side of " Holdgait" for 80 years; and in 1578 made a grant of $2\frac{3}{4}$ roods of land on the south side " Nether Oldgaiet," between Baye's Lands on the east and the water of the Wansbeck on the west. which must, Hodgson thinks, be the terrace and garden which belonged to the house in which Lord Collingwood occasionally resided in the street.

Howard Terrace is a fine row of modern erections, the dwellings being those of the tradesmen and others of the town. It faces Cottingwood and the fields to the north.

Dacre Street is a comparatively new street, and includes some handsome dwellings, with extensive garden grounds in front. It is situated near Howard Terrace, and enters from the Dam Side, at the foot of the town. In Dacre

Street is "Dacre Castle," a modern building, the residence of Mr. Joseph Jobling; "The Manse," in which resides the Rev. A. H Drysdale, M.A.; and "Winton House," which is occupied by Councillor T. R. Miller.

Manchester Lane enters from Newgate Street, and leads to Dacre Street, Union Street, Well Way, and Howard Terrace.

Bullersgreen is the name of a small township adjoining the north-west boundary of the town, where the road turns off at the head of Newgate Street to Mitford. On a plan of Morpeth in 1603, the west end of the street was closed with a gateway. The name was some years since Bowlesgreen, and is believed to have been the bowling green of between three and four centuries ago.

COMMON LANDS.

The Common, known as Morpeth Common, lies on the south-west side of the parish church, and comprises over 400 acres. It belongs to the Corporation. which pays no rent or acknowledgment of any kind for it. The burgesses and bailiffs used to ride the boundaries annually on St. Mark's day, April 25th, when the chief magistrates gave a piece of plate to be run for by horses of the burgesses. In 1766, the Corporation, under the direction of two stewards from each of the various companies then existing, improved the Common, and had the ground hedged in and cultivated, and Hodgson also mentions that in 1831, "a house was built upon it, adjoining the churchyard, for a watchman to reside in and preserve the graves from being robbed by that most odious race of criminals— resurrection men. Each resident freeman and free-brother of the several companies, according to the bye-laws of the Corporation in 1831, had the privilege of pasturing two cows upon the Common."

The High Stanners and the Low Stanners are two plots of unenclosed ground by the side of the river. The High Stanners is on the west side of the river, between the entrance to the Mitford road and the Oldgate foot bridge, and is in the hands of the Corporation, and used as a place of amusement and recreation for the people. The Low Stanners is on the north side of the first turn of the river below the town. Persons sentenced to death were at one time executed there.

The Terrace, a square plot of enclosed ground, is on the north bank of the river, almost adjoining the Presbyterian Church at the back. There is a walk around it, which is encircled with trees. It is seated in the summer, when it affords a pleasant promenade for the public. It is also held by the Corporation.

THE POLICE STATION

is a neat modern erection, situate in Chantry Place. Within the station are police-offices, residence for officers, and cells. Attached is the residence of the Police Superintendent, Mr. Mark Young.

THE POST OFFICE.

at Morpeth is the centre of a large district, and mails are daily despatched from it to Blyth, Bedlington, Newbiggin, Cresswell, Hartburn, Rothbury, &c., and mail carts arrive every evening from these places, in time for the north and south mails. The office is very conveniently situated on the west side of the Market place. The accommodation provided in the establishment is of a fairly satisfactory character. There is telegraphic communication from 7 a.m. to 8 p.m. on week days, and from 7·30 to 10 a.m. on Sundays. Besides the stamp and letter department, money order and post office savings bank business is also conducted during certain hours. The post office is open for the sale of stamps, and for the posting of letters north and south, until 9·55 p.m. every week-day. Mr. T. W. Knight is the postmaster.

BANKS.

THE Saving's Bank was established in 1816, under the patronage and trust of the Duke of Portland, Sir C. Monck, Bart., and W. Ord, Esq., M.P. The number of trustees were increased; and in 1829, a piece of ground on the Back Riggs was purchased, and a neat and commodious building erected on it, in which the business still continues to be transacted.—The North-Eastern Banking Company, formerly the Alnwick and County Bank, have splendid premises in Newgate Street; Messrs. Lambton and Co's Bank occupies a capital site on the north side of the Market place; Messrs. Hodgkin, Barnett, Pease, and Spence, have also their bank in Newgate Street, while Messrs. Woods and Company have a branch establishment in Bridge Street.

WATER SUPPLY.

THE Water Works at the Allery Banks were made in 1820, by Mr. Thomas King. The reservoir is situated at the Allery Banks, and the water brought in pipes to the lower part of the town from it. There are also water works at Tranwell, and feeders to a storage reservoir on Morpeth Common. Mr. Young, in boring for his New Ærated Water Works, came on a spring of excellent water, the overflow of which he turned into a fountain for the full benefit of the public, and which has proved of most excellent service for the public in general, especially those residing at the lower part of the town. There is also an excellent well of good water at Beggar's Lane for the dwellers at the high end of the town.

THE GAS WORKS.

are situated near the Low Stanners, and are the property of a public company, established in 1832, by whom the town is supplied. Previous to the passing of the Corporation Reform Act the town was almost in entire darkness. It is recorded that, "on the 19th of November, 1833, the Morpeth Gas Company commenced lighting the town with gas, to the great satisfaction of the inhabitants."

EDUCATIONAL AND OTHER INSTITUTIONS.

SCHOOLS.

IN addition to the Royal Grammar School already referred to, there are the following educational establishments: St. James' School, Newgate Street, master, Mr. W. Bullock; St. George's School, Cottingwood Lane, Mr. James Fergusson; Boarding School, Newgate Street, Mrs. Armstrong; Ladies' Seminary, Newgate Street, Miss Morton; Boarding and Day School, Miss Purdy, Dacre Street; Ladies' Seminary, Newgate Street, Mrs. and Miss Paton; Borough Schools, Dacre Street. Misses Lillie and Wright; St. Robert's School, Oldgate Street,

THE MECHANICS' INSTITUTION.

RESPECTING the history of this useful and popular institution, we quote the following from the Jubilee sketch, issued in 1875, by Mr. James Fergusson, the secretary:—

The establishment of a Mechanical and Scientific Institution in the town of Morpeth was one of the immediate results of that educational movement which issued in practical deeds in the year 1823. A number of mechanics and others met at Mr. Lackenby's on the 21st of February, 1825, for the purpose of taking into consideration the propriety of establishing a Mechanical and Scientific Institution in the town of Morpeth At that preliminary meeting a committee was appointed to carry the project forward. The members of that committee (not one of whom is alive at this date) were:—Thomas Walker, John Jackson, Robert Blakey, Thomas Bowman, Peter Blair, William Robson, William Wilson, jun., Richard Lewins, William Wilson, senr. Michael Clarke, and J. A. Thompson. They issued a circular, dated the 28th of February, setting forth in glowing language the aims and advantages of such an institution, and "respectfully requesting a general meeting of the inhabitants of the town and neighbourhood at the Town Hall, on the 17th day of March."

The meeting thus summoned was duly held, and was presided over by Mr. Benjamin Woodman, senior bailiff. Among the seven resolutions unanimously agreed to, the most important was as follows:— "That a Mechanical and Scientific Institution for the town of Morpeth and its neighbourhood, principally for the use of mechanics and labouring people, is highly desirable, and cannot fail to give importance to the town, and to confer a great benefit on those for whom it is instituted."

The first committee appointed to frame rules, solicit subscriptions and donations, &c , were:—John Watson, Thomas Walker, William Haswell, Thomas King, George Grey, Gibson Kyle, William Beldon, Michael Bates, Michael Clarke, William Bell, William Stephenson, Thos. Bowman, J. A Thompson, John Manners, Peter Blair, William Robson, William Wilson, Richard Lewins, William Wilson, Robert Hall; Robert Blakey and Anthony Charlton, secretaries; and John Jackson, treasurer.

Rules were prepared, books purchased, and a room engaged without loss of time. The library was formally opened on the 1st of June, 1825, in two rooms situated on the east side of the Scotch Arms Yard, immediately behind the old Town Hall. The rooms were on the second floor of a building that occupied the site of the present Corn Exchange. At the end of the first year, the committee reported that the institution possessed 574 volumes—a few of which had been presented during the year. They had purchased 549 volumes, an electrical machine, and certain other philosophical instruments for £208 19s. 6d. The whole amount of subscriptions and donations for the first year amounted to £244 4s. 2d. The foundation of the institution was the occasion of a large amount of rancour and ill-feeling, and evoked considerable opposition—not the less determined because it did a great part of its work from behind a hedge. It is to the credit of the founders and early supporters of the institution that they held on the even tenor of their way, regardless of the ridicule and personal abuse of fellow townsmen, who had not the manliness to appear at the public meeting in the Town Hall, and there, in the face of the inhabitants generally, state their objections to the enterprise that was about to be undertaken. After such hostility, it was no wonder that the committee at the end of the second year expressed themselves "fully convinced of the stability and usefulness of the institution; and bore testimony to the good effects already produced by it."

The institution existed for ten years before any attempt was made to establish classes for the benefit of the younger members. The initiative was then taken by the late Mr. W. Creighton, surgeon and apothecary, who, in 1835, began a class for the study of chemistry, and in the following year organised one for the study of languages upon the Hamiltonian system. In the early reports frequent mention is made of the harmony and unanimity that prevailed among the members—the secret no doubt of its bearing up against the depression that would otherwise have attended a declining fortune of nine years' duration. The only question that seriously disturbed the peace of

the institution during that time was the admission of the Waverley
Novels in 1830. A very large majority of the members voted for
their introduction, but it was strenuously opposed by "some members
anxiously desirous for the welfare of the institution." In these circumstances, "the committee consented to admit them, with an express
stipulation that no other productions of a like kind should ever be
allowed to enter the library," and under a regulation that one penny
per volume should be charged each time of issue, thus establishing a
fund "by which the expense of this somewhat objectionable acquisi-
tion to the property of the society would be defrayed without infrin-
ging on the regular contributions." Two years later, the committee
reports, "that the accession of these novels has not in any measure
diminished the general desire that has always existed among the
members to study productions containing more practical information."
In 1838, the rule prohibiting the introduction of novels was rescinded,
and in the following year the committee reported that they had purchased a new set of the Waverley Novels, the original series having
become utterly dilapidated through being "more frequently and generally read than any other class of books in the library;" and what
was more significant still, they had bought eight volumes of new
novels besides. And yet the committee tried hard to dam back the
rising tide. The charge of one penny per volume was retained, and a
resolution passed by the committee that not more than five pounds
should at one time be expended on works of fiction. Both of these
have disappeared from the minutes of the institution.

The original plan of keeping open three nights a week only was
continued down to June, 1847, when by resolution of the members
the rooms were opened for six nights. Like almost every other
material change introduced, this experiment is reported on unfavour-
ably, giving rise to the supposition that there must have been an
influential party in the committee who, on principle, "opposed all
improvements." Nevertheless the plan was continued, and it naturally
raised the question of introducing newspapers; for members could
not go there night after night without craving for some information
respecting the news of the day. This desire was partially supplied
in 1848 by newspapers being obtained in loan from gentlemen in the
town; in 1851 the *Times* was taken in, and in 1852 a news room was
formally added as one of the departments of the institution. In
this connection, and to a generation in whose time the newspaper is
ubiquitous, it may not be uninteresting nor uninstructive to quote
from the report of 1852 a short paragraph giving some idea of the
general dread of the "political working man" that must have prevailed even so late as a quarter of a century ago. The report says
that "the originators of Mechanics' Institutions wisely considered it
unjustifiable to appropriate any portion of their funds to the pur-
chasing of newspapers, and used an indispensable circumspection in
rigidly excluding all discussion of matters touching politics or the-
ology. But after the lapse of twenty-seven years, the time has
arrived when the free expression of opinion, then so much dreaded,
is not only tolerated, but it has become habitual, and it is not to be

controlled; and when the working man *will* consult the newspaper and if denied the use of it in the reading room of the Mechanics Institution, he is tempted to seek for it elsewhere."

The next marked event in its history was the holding of an Exhibition in the spring of 1856 —the managing committee of which were : Messrs. H. Robinson, J. R. Hardy, James Hood, W. Wilson, R. Leckie, W Creighton, W. N. Blair, W. Grahamsley, W. Wilkinson, D. F. Wilson, W. Jobling, W. Duncan, and W. R. Watson. The exhibition was open for three weeks, during which time twelve lectures were delivered by gentlemen of the town and neighbourhood, and three concerts were given. It was a decided success.

During the time the new Town Hall was being built, the institution had to find temporary accommodation in various parts of the town. On the 29th of September, 1870, the institution formally entered on the occupation of the new rooms, and the event was celebrated with some *eclat*. According to previous arrangement, the annual meeting of the Northern Union of Mechanics was held in the new Town Hall (by which meeting it was formally opened), under the presidency of the Right Honourable Sir George Grey, Bart. The furnishing of the new rooms cost £135.

Few changes took place in the managing officers of the society. From its foundation till 1871 the secretaries were changed annually ; and at first it had been the intention to elect a new treasurer each year also. This had been found inconvenient, as the following is a list of the treasurers from its beginning :—John Jackson, 1825-6 ; Richard Lewins, 1826-7 ; William Clarke, 1827-8 ; Edward Robson, 1828-9 ; Thomas Bowman, 1829-54 ; William Creighton, 1854-70 ; William James Atkinson, 1870—   Mr. William Wilson, was librarian from its establishment till March, 1865. Mr. Wilson was succeeded by Mr Charles Lea, and he having retired, Mr. James Fergusson was elected in June, 1869.

In 1871 the constitution of the society was entirely remodelled on the most liberal basis--the management of its affairs being so placed, by means of the ballot, in the hands of the members, that they can give free expression to their opinions without any dread of unpleasantness arising from giving personal offence. As might be expected, the occupation of the new rooms in the Town Hall, and other circumstances incidentally connected therewith, helped to give an impetus to the institution, and it is believed by its oldest members that it never was more prosperous than at the present time.

The institution has a large room in the Town Hall as its library, whilst an admirably adapted apartment of the hall. of spacious dimensions and excellently lighted, is employed as a reading room, and is abundantly supplied with the leading daily and weekly newspapers, both local and national. The extent to which both the library and the reading room are patronised by the members is most satisfactory, and the beneficial influence of the institution is generally acknowledged. In the library there are above 4,000 volumes, embracing the standard and most recently published works in the various classes :— (A) History and Biography ; (B) Mental, Moral, and Political Science ; (C) Voyages, Travels, and Geography ; (D) Industrial and Fine Arts Criticism ; (E) Mathematics, Physical Science, and Natural Philosophy ; (F) Fiction ; (G) Periodicals and Miscellaneous ; (H) Poetry. In the course of the winter months, a series of useful lectures, scientific and microscopical exhibitions, and concerts, are given in the Town Hall, promoted by the institution, which are very numerously patronised as a rule.

In 1874, the following with other books were presented to the institution :—" The History of Charles the XII.," a late translation, printed and sold by S. Wilkinson, Morpeth, 1807, and " The Abriged Statistical History of Scotland," by William Woodman, Esq., the former being a copy of the first book printed in Morpeth. In 1871, there were presented to it by the Barony of Morpeth, in memory of the late Earl of Carlisle, who was for many years its patron, 75 volumes of valuable and costly works in science and art, and a large telescope and microscope. Among the books are a unique collection of the original editions of works written by authors who were natives of Morpeth, including " Turner's Herbal " (black letter), published in the year 1561. There are in the library 127 volumes, published by the Record Commission, which were formerly in the custody of " The Morpeth Library," and from its discontinuance till May, 1874, in the office of the Town Clerk of this borough, and have been deposited in this institution by the authority of the Secretary of state for the Home Department. The fiftieth annual meeting of the institution was held on Thursday evening, July 8th, 1875, in the Reading Room of the institution at the Town Hall, the Mayor (Mr. R. Wilkinson) presiding. The secretary read the fiftieth annual report, which showed that 55 new members had joined the institute during the past year, and the number on the roll was 253, a much larger number than was ever reported at an annual meeting before. The income for the year had been £175 9s., 1d., and the expenditure £149 9s. 8d. The Jubilee of the institution was celebrated by holding an exhibition of works of art. The proceedings connected with the celebration commenced on the evening of the 9th of September, 1875, when an interesting exhibition was opened by a public meeting in the Town Hall of the borough, at which the Rector of Morpeth presided, and addresses were given by Mr. Thomas Burt, M.P., Sir Arthur Monck, Bart., M.P., and the Rev. E. Lawson, J.P, Longhirst Hall, after which the exhibition was declared open. The exhibition was a very large and extensive one, occupying the Town Hall, the Corn Exchange, and the ante-room of the hall. It comprised the following classes :—

A.—Pictures in oil, water, and chalk. Prints, old, curious, and rare. Statuary.
B.--Literature—Books—by Morpeth authors, or printed in Morpeth : old, rare, or curious ; illustrativ. of Local History or character ; old Newspapers, Fly Sheets, Hand-bills, &c., possessing a local interest, &c.
C.--Coins, Medals. and Specimens of Artistic work, in the precious and other metals.
D.—Specimens of Art and Curiosities from Eastern or Uncivilized countries.
E.—Preserved Specimens of Natural History.
F.—Pottery, old, modern, home, and foreign.
G.—Miscellaneous objects, which could not be conveniently classed under any of the foregoing heads.

The sub-committees appointed to superintend the classes were as follows :—(A) Messrs. E. Garvie, J. Hann, and C. Pringle ; (B) Messrs. W. Davidson, B.A., and J. Cocks ; (C) Messrs. W. M. Boag, and George Jeffrey ; D) Messrs. W. J. Atkinson, and Thomas Hudson ; (E) Messrs. F. E. Schofield and W. Duncan ; (F) Messrs. J. Haswell, R. W. Dixon, and Fred. Barrow, Esq., M.R.C.S. ; (G) Messrs. John Davison, T. W. Middlemiss, and Charles Alderson.

The collection of articles remained open from the 9th to the 18th of September, during which time it was very largely patronised. Amateur and promenade concerts were given on certain evenings ; and on Wednesday evening, the 15th September, a public meeting was held in the large hall, the Mayor presiding, when an address was given by Major Duncan, R.A., and votes of thanks were accorded to all the gentlemen who had contributed to the success of the Jubilee proceedings.

THE MORPETH YOUNG MEN'S MUTUAL IMPROVEMENT SOCIETY (undenominational) meets on Monday evenings during the winter months, in the ante-room of the Town Hall.

MORPETH DISPENSARY.

Is situate in Bell's Yard, Bridge Street, the object of the institution being to afford medical attendance and medicine gratuitously to indigent persons. The medical staff consists of four duly qualified gentlemen, who comprise the medical committee, and a house surgeon, the gentleman occupying that position at the present being Mr. J. H. Gosling. The number of patients who were admitted to the benefit of this useful charity in 1883 was 449. Mr. G. O. Wright is the hon.-sec., and Mr. Greenwood the treasurer of the institution.

ALMS HOUSES.

ON the 16th of August, 1839, a meeting of the inhabitants of Morpeth was held to consider what should be done with the old Workhouse, which had been for some time unoccupied, when it was resolved to convert it into an alms house for aged persons not receiving parish relief. A subscription was immediately commenced, and the building was soon after altered in the manner proposed. The alms houses are in Cottingwood Lane.

NEWSPAPERS.

The Morpeth Herald is the only newspaper issued in the town, and is printed on Friday evenings. The office is in Bridge Street. The paper is well-established. It has a weekly circulation of about 6,000 and is read by the agriculturists in the widely scattered farm-steads of Central Northumberland, as well as by the residents in the locality of Morpeth.

The Newcastle Daily Chronicle, the Daily Journal, Northern Daily Express, and other daily newspapers, have a large circle of readers in the district. There are also a large number of weekly and monthly papers sold in the town and district.

THE Corn, Cattle, and Provision Markets are held on the Wednesday of each week. Cattle and Horse Fairs are held in March and October. There are also half-yearly Hirings for hinds and general servants.

VOLUNTEERS.—There is a respectable Company of Volunteers at Morpeth, known as the B. Company 1st Battalion Northumberland Fusiliers. Mr. Jas. Haswell is captain; Mr. W. Wilkinson is lieutenant, and Mr. N. I. Wright the secretary. Mr. John Donnelly is the drill-instructor.

AKENSIDE, the poet, wrote the first edition of his " Pleasures of Imagination " at Morpeth, in 1770, and thus expresses the lasting influence the delightful scenery of the Wansbeck had upon his mind :—

> Oh ye Northumbrian shades, which overlook
> The rocky pavement, and the mossy falls
> Of solitary Wansbeck's limpid stream,
> How gladly I recall your well known seats,
> Beloved of old, and that delightful time,
> When, all alone, for many a summer's day,
> I wandered through your calm recesses, led
> In silence by some powerful hand unseen.

> *　　*　　*　　*　　*

> Nor will I e'er forget you ; nor shall e'er
> The graver tasks of manhood, or th' advice
> Of vulgar wisdom, move me to disdain
> Those studies which possessed me in the dawn
> Of life, and fixed the colour of my mind
> For every future year.

MEMORIALS OF THE PAST.

THE OLD CORPORATION.

PRIOR to the passing and coming into operation of the Municipal Reform Act, the Corporation of Morpeth was styled "The Corporation of the Bailiffs and Burgesses of the Borough of Morpeth." The whole corporate body of Morpeth at that time consisted of seven companies or fraternities, which were also called trades or crafts, and each of these companies comprised an alderman and an indefinite number of free brothers and free burgesses. These companies were :—The Merchants and Tailors; the Tanners; the Fullers and Dyers, including Carvers and Hatters; the Smiths, Saddlers, and Armourers; the Cordwainers; the Weavers; the Skinners and Glovers, and Butchers. The Alderman had to be a burgess, and was chosen annually by the brothers and burgesses of the respective company over the meetings of which he presided. He also sat upon the bench at the several courts held by the lord of the manor, and audited the accounts of the bailiffs, &c. Each alderman kept a key of the Town's Hutch; he had charge of the box of his company during his period of office, and under him were two deputies called Proctors, who were eligible only out of the brothers or free-burgesses of their own company. The aldermen could not open the boxes under their charges without the consent of the proctor, who kept the key, nor had the bailiffs who were the guardians of the Hutch, to have access to it, without the consent of the whole of the aldermen, who had to be present with their keys when it had to be opened. The free-brothers obtained their freedom and privileges by birth or servitude. The privileges to which brothers were entitled were :—To follow the trade of their respective companies, and to take apprentices; to vote for aldermen and proctors; in making bye-laws and transacting the business of their respective companies; to vote in the election of burgesses; to have the same number of stints on the common as the burgesses had, &c. The free-burgesses were also called freemen and were chosen out of the body of brothers. They had all the privileges of the brothers, and in addition thereto they had the power to make bye-laws for the body corporate, and to vote at the election of members to serve the town in Parliament, and of masters and ushers of the school of Edward the Sixth. At the election of Officers to preside annually over the Corporation in those times, each of the several companies made a return to the lord of the manor, or his steward, at a court leet, of two belonging to his own company for bailiffs, one for a sergeant-at-mace, one for fish and flesh lookers, one for ale-tasters, two for bread weighers, and two for constables, out of which the lord or steward selected two bailiffs, one sergeant-at-mace, two fish and flesh lookers, two ale-tasters and bread weighers, and four constables, and swears each of them into his respective office. The ale-tasters and bread weighers of one year were always returned by the juries, the fish and flesh lookers for the next. The bailiffs were for the time the head officers of the Corporation. There were with the burgesses, the patrons and governors of the school of King Edward the Sixth, let its lands, and received and accounted for their rents to the master and usher. The sergeant-at-mace was the servant of the bailiffs. He kept the mace, summoned the aldermen to inform their companies of the meetings; was the cryer, and delivered all summonses of the borough courts. The Arms of the ancient De Merlays are a castle, with eight birds on a border. The original grant of the Grammar School in the Record office is emblazoned with the arms of Dacre, with seven quarterings, the shield of the town of Morpeth, and various other armorial devices.

ANCIENT EXCLUSIVE RIGHTS.—On the 6th of April, 1746, it was resolved by the Corporation, " That none but a free-man or brother shall exercise the trade of a whitesmith, blacksmith, saddler, armourer, or hardwareman, within

the borough." The guild books contain many similar resolutions respecting other trades.—" The toon's a' wor
awn ! "—*Ola saying.*

COTTINGWOOD.—The land upon which the Asylum is
erected and surrounding it is called Cottingwood. In 1604,
there were 284 acres. which the bailiffs and burgesses held
of William Lord Howard. They afterwards rented and
used it as a common. During the great plague in 1665,
the people of Morpeth are said to have encamped upon it,
and such of them that died were buried in a small field
adjoining Holborn, at the foot of the Quarry Bank.

HANGMAN'S LAND.— The burgesses and community of
Morpeth. by deed without date, devised to Patrick, the
hangman of Morpeth, a rood of land, out of which the
bridge and chapel had an annual rent of 4s. They also let
it again in 1326, and Hangman Land is mentioned in 1463
and 1465, in the annals of Morpeth.

EMINENT MEN.

THE town and neighbourhood of Morpeth is associated with
the names of several men of distinguished attainments in
literature and the sciences.

WILLIAM TURNER, A.M. and M.D., the celebrated botanist
and ornithologist, was a native of Morpeth. He was
educated at Cambridge, became a very zealous Reformer,
was imprisoned by Bishop Gardner, but he was " let loose,"
and proceeded to Ferrara, in Italy, where he took his de-
gree of M.D. He returned to England in the reign of
Elizabeth, and wrote " an Herbal," the complete edition of
which, in 1568, was printed at Cologne. Turner first gave
names to many English plants, and the publication of this
work was received with considerable appreciation ; it un-
doubtedly possessed great merit; he also wrote several works
on divinity; and treatises on birds, fishes, plants, stones,
metals, &c. He died in London on the 7th of July, 1568.

JOHN HORSLEY, M.A. and F.R.S., a learned antiquary,
was a native of Northumberland, and succeeded Dr. Harle
as the minister of the Presbyterian Church of Morpeth,
in December, 1729. He died in December, 1731, at the
age of 46. He was the author of a valuable and learned

work, " Britannia Romanæ; or, the Roman Antiquities of Great Britain," which was not published until after his death.

THE REV. ROBERT MORRISON, D.D., the great Chinese scholar and missionary, was born on the 5th of January, 1782, at Bullersgreen, Morpeth. When he was about three years old, his parents went to Newcastle to live. At the age of 16 he joined the Presbyterian Church in High Bridge, Newcastle, and subsequently during his intervals of leisure and work-hours, he entered upon biblical and classical studies, acquired some knowledge of Hebrew, Latin, and Greek, and learned to write shorthand with ease. He was admitted to the Independent College at Hoxton in 1803; a year after his services were accepted by the London Missionary Society, and in the College at Gosport he began the study of Chinese, and soon mastered the language as to be able to read and write it. After studying medicine and astronomy he left for China in 1807. He proceeded with his missionary labours with great success, published several works in Chinese, and his great work, "The Dictionary of the Chinese Language." He died at Canton, August 1, 1834, in his fifty-third year.

THE REV. JOHN HODGSON, M.R.S.L., the author of the History of Northumberland, was born at Shap, in 1779, and received his earliest education at Brampton. In 1827, he was appointed to the living at the Parsonage of Hartburn, about seven miles west from Morpeth, in the valley of the Wansbeck, and there he wrote his comprehensive history, which is published in six volumes.

LUKE CLENNELL, a celebrated painter and wood engraver, was born on the 30th of March, 1781, at Ulgham, a small village on the south bank of the river Line, about five miles north-east of Morpeth. He was bound apprentice to Thomas Bewick, of Newcastle. After serving his time, he proceeded to London, where he acquitted himself with great credit, his wood-cuts securing for him the gold medal of the Society of Arts and £100. He also received one hundred and fifty guineas from the British Institution, for the best picture of the " Final Charge of the Life Guards at Waterloo." He died in February, 1840, at Newcastle, in the lunatic asylum, his mind having given way in 1817.

PLACES OF INTEREST IN THE DISTRICT.

IN the neighbourhood of Morpeth are Bolam House, the seat of Lord Decies; Wallington Hall, of Sir C. Trevelyan, bart.; Capheaton Hall, of Sir John Swinburne, bart.; Belsay Hall, of Sir A. E. Middleton, bart., M P. The townships, villages, and hamlets in the neighbourhood include:—Benridge, a mile to the north of Mitford; Bothal Demesne; Ashington and Sheepwash, 4½ miles north-east of Morpeth (there are very extensive collieries at Ashington, employing some hundreds of miners); Catchburn, 2 miles south of Morpeth; the Gubeon Farm, at the West end of Morpeth High Common; Edington; High and Low Highlaws; Hepscott, formerly Heppescottes, on the eastern boundary of the parish of Morpeth, 2 miles from the town; Hebron 3 miles north by west from Morpeth; Longhorsley, 7 miles north-west from Morpeth; Parkhouse and Stobhill, three quarters of a mile south-east of Morpeth; Molesdon; Newton Park; Newton Underwood; Nunriding; Newminster Abbey, where the Kennels of the Morpeth Foxhounds are; Old Moor, 4½ miles north-east of Morpeth, and a mile from Longhirst; Pegswood, 2 miles north-east of Morpeth, a large colliery village, formerly called Pegsworth; Pigdon; Spittle Hill, 2½ miles west of Morpeth; Throphill; Shadfen, on the south west side of the river, a mile from Morpeth; Shilvington, 5 miles south-west from Morpeth; Tranwell, 2 miles south-west from Morpeth; Twizell, 6¼ miles from Morpeth to the south west, on the Blyth river.

BOTHAL CASTLE.

BOTHAL.

A very pleasant, though rather long walk through the Chapel wood, leads from Morpeth to Bothal, a very delightfully situated village, about three miles to the east of Morpeth, and pleasantly placed on the north bank of the river Wansbeck. St. Andrew's Church is said to be the work of the 14th century, and is of stone, containing a chancel, nave, aisles, porch, and has an open belfry at the west end, with three bells. The register dates from 1678. The rectory is at Sheepwash. The living is the gift of the Duke of Portland, and is held by the Hon. and Rev. William Charles Ellis, M.A., of Balliol College, Oxford. The Rev. John Lightfoot is the curate. There are charities of £2 yearly value bequeathed to the poor of Bothal by the Rev. Mr. Stafford, who was Rector of Bothal in 1716. There is a fine monument of alabaster to Baron Ogle and his lady, and in some of the windows of the church are remants of stained glass, and armorial bearings are placed in various parts of the sacred edifice.

BOTHAL CASTLE stands upon a green knoll adjacant to the church, and is still an imposing monument of feudal grandeur. The river Wansbeck rushes close by to the south of the castle, and the scenery of the locality is very picturesque and charming, and is a favourite resort of picnic parties. The Duke of Portland is the lord of the barony. Regarding the castle it is recorded that "in 1344 Robert Bertram obtained a licence from Edward the Third to make a castle of his manor house." The castle next passed into the hands of Sir Robert Ogle and remained in the possession of the family until the death of the Duke of Newcastle, Earl of Ogle, who met his death at the battle of Marsden Moor. The castle then descended by the female line to the Portland family.

CHOPPINGTON is four miles east by south of Morpeth, on the Blyth and Tyne Railway. Scotland Gate is about half a mile from the station, and Guide Post about a mile distant. The population in 1871 was 4,150.

MITFORD CASTLE.

MITFORD

Is a parish, 2¼ miles to the west of Morpeth, and is situated on the Wansbeck and the Font, both of which are spanned by stone bridges. Directly overlooking the village of Mitford, built upon the hill on the north side of the road, is a handsome modern hall, Spittle Hill, the residence of Thomas Gray, Esq., of Newcastle-upon-Tyne. Passing through the village, and up the steep hill, the visitor will turn down the first carriage road on the left, which leads to the Castle, Church, and Parsonage. Here are the ruins of a very ancient castle, like Morpeth, on the south side of the river Wansbeck. The locality has been the residence of the Bertram family and their descendants, from the time of the Conquest, at which time the Bertrams became connected by marriage with the heiress of the Mitford family. On the south side are the ruined walls of the Castle, as represented in the engraving. The stronghold was built between 1150 and 1170, by William Bertram, the founder of Brinkburn Priory. In 1212 the castle, as well as the town, was burnt by King John, when returning from his crusade against Alexander, King of Scotland, who asserted his claim to Northumberland. The castle is represented to have been taken by Alexander in 1318, when it was dismantled and spoiled.

The modern building, Mitford Castle, is a noble erection, and can be seen from the heights surrounding the old ruin, about a quarter of a mile to the west. The lord of the manor, Colonel John Philip Osbaldeston Mitford resides here.

The Church of St. Mary was an ancient stone building, in the Norman and early English styles, and had a chancel, transept, nave, porch, and bell-turret, with two bells. The register dates from 1667. The living is a discharged vicarage, in the gift of the Bishop of Durham, and held by the Rev. Thomas Austen Holcroft, M.A. A parish school for boys and girls and a Sunday school is held in the church. The church has, however been entirely rebuilt, at the expense of Colonel J. P. Osbaldeston Mitford. The plans for the restoration were prepared by Mr. Johnson, architect, Newcastle; and the work of erection has been executed by

Messrs. Waterston, Morpeth. The church, now complete, is the same early English chancel, the same nave lengthened by the addition of a fourth arch, and extended by a south aisle, engaged with the Mitford chapel, and a tower engaged with the nave, which is made loftier and more imposing by the original walls having been heightened to admit of clerestory windows. Exclusive of the tower, the length of the nave is about 59 feet, while that of the original Norman nave must have been about 73 feet. The new south aisle is eight feet wide, while that of the Norman erection would be about a foot more, and an aisle of similar width on the north side gives 73 feet by 43 feet as the dimensions of the original nave and aisles.

COCKLE PARK TOWER.

FROM three to four miles north of Morpeth, in the chapelry of Hebron, is Cockle Park Tower, or Cockley Tower, an ancient peel, now converted into a farm house, on a farm called Bubbley Mires. Grose gives a fine view of it in his Antiquities, as it appeared in the year 1774. It belonged, in the time of Edward the First, to the Bertrams, but is now the property of the Duke of Portland, to whose ancestors it devolved, in 1734, by the same succession as Bothal Castle.

LONGHIRST.

LONGHIRST is a township and village, about three miles north of Morpeth, on the North-Eastern Railway. Longhirst Hall is the residence of W. E. Lawson, Esq. A handsome and pleasantly situated new church was opened at Longhirst, on Tuesday, September 14th, 1875. The edifice is built in the early English style of architecture, with stained glass windows to match. Messrs. Waterston, of Morpeth, were the builders. There is a porch at the north side and a tower and spire, the height of which is 100 feet. The interior of the building consists of a nave, side aisles, transepts, and chancel. The architect is Mr. Bloomfield of London, and the building, which cost £5,000, was built at the sole expense of the late Rev. Edward Lawson, of Longhirst Hall, who was licensed curate of the new church by the Bishop. The Rev. A. Field is the preacher.

COCKLE PARK TOWER.

BRINKBURN PRIORY.

OF this priory, the Church only remains almost entire, and presents fine examples of late Norman and Transitional architecture. It occupies a very secluded position, in the valley of the Coquet, five miles east of Rothbury. It was formed by William Bertram, in the reign of Henry I., for the Augustine canons. A modern castellated building is erected near the Abbey, and is the residence of C. H. Cadogan, Esq., J.P.

HARTBURN is a delightful little village, between eight and nine miles west by north from Morpeth. The church is a large building, with a square tower, and a flat roof, supported by rows of pillars. The Rev. Beilby Porteous Hodgson, B.A., is the Vicar of Hartburn.

NETHERWITTON is about eight miles west north-west from Morpeth. The river Font flows through the village. The Church of St. Giles is a small, but compact ancient edifice. It is in the vicarage of Hartburn, and the present minister is the Rev. Mr. Hicks, M.A. Nunnykirk, the seat of W. Orde, Esq., is about a mile and a half north-west from Netherwitton.

WHALTON is situated about seven miles south-west of Morpeth, and about two miles from Meldon Station on the Wansbeck Valley Railway. The Rev. W. Walker is the Rector of the parish. Meldon is $6\frac{1}{2}$ miles west of Morpeth. Meldon Park is the residence of John Cookson, Esq., J.P.

NETHERTON is $3\frac{1}{2}$ miles to the south of Morpeth, and $1\frac{1}{2}$ miles east from Netherton Station on the North-Eastern Railway. The Reformatory School for boys, for Northumberland and Durham is at Netherton.

BEDLINGTON is five miles from Morpeth to the south-east. The village is situated on the highest land in the parish, and commands a view of the German ocean and the out lying districts. The Church of St. Cuthbert is a stone Gothic building, consisting of semi-circular nave, chancel, with tower, clock, and bells. The living is held by the Rev. C. T. Whitley, M.A., of St. John's College, Cambridge.

ALNWICK AND WARKWORTH.

THE town of Alnwick is situated on the south side of the river Aln, from whence it derives its name. It is about 21 miles north of Morpeth by rail. The castle was built in the 12th century by Eustace de Vescy. The barony came into the possession of Henry, Lord Percy, in 1309, and the chief portions of the noble residence were the work of the second Lord Henry. The architectural appearance of the barbican is very striking, the parapets being surmounted with stone figures representing warriors in various positions. The population of Alnwick is over seven thousand.

The village of Warkworth is situated a short distance from the mouth of the Coquet. The Harbour is about a mile and a half off Amble. The Castle is in the hands of the house of Percy. It is picturesquely situated on the banks of the Coquet, and can be clearly seen from the railway when passing Warkworth. The prison, towers, and appartments attached, have for the most part fallen into complete decay, and, with the walls, are now in ruins.